TRENCHERMAN'S

GW00703105

Best Inns ∉
in the Eastern Counties

Compiled by: Michael Campbell
Edited by: James Lawrence

CONTENTS

Published by
Bracken Publishing
Bracken House, 199a Holt Road
Cromer, Norfolk NR27 9JN

ISBN 1 871614 16 3

Printed by Broadgate Printers, Aylsham, Norfolk.

April 1993

CHAMPION BEER of BRITAIN - 1990/91

This is to certify that

Adnams Bitter

was judged to be

CHAMPION
Standard Bitter
of Britain

at the
GREAT BRITISH BEER
FESTIVAL
BRIGHTON, AUGUST 1990

John M. Cryne
National Chairman

From Suffolk's Oldest Brewery Britain's Finest Beer

SOLE BAY BREWERY · SOUTHWOLD · SUFFOLK IP18 6JW · TELEPHONE SOUTHWOLD (0502) 722424

Important

Please note:-

1. Dishes quoted from menus are examples only, and not necessarily available at all times.

2. The listing of brewers' beers and lagers does not mean that the full range is necessarily available.

3. Prices, where quoted, may alter during the currency of this guide.

4. Every effort is made to ensure accuracy, but inevitably circumstances change and errors and omissions may occur. Therefore the publisher cannot accept liability for any consequences arising therefrom.

5. This is a selection: it is not claimed that all the best inns and pubs are featured.

6. Your comments about any establishment, favourable or not, are particularly welcome. Correspondents who especially impress the editor will receive a complimentary copy of the next edition.

7. Special note to publicans: if your house is not included, please do not be offended! The area covered is very large and time limited. If you serve good food in pleasant surrounds, please write and we will visit you.

FURTHER COPIES OF THIS OR OUR OTHER GUIDES MAY BE OBTAINED BY WRITING TO:-

Bracken Publishing
Bracken House
199a Holt Road
Cromer
Norfolk NR27 9JN

Enclose payment as follows:-

Eastern Counties (Inns & Pubs)	£4.00
Eastern Counties (Hotels & Restaurants)	£3.50
Cotswolds, Thames Valley & Chilterns (Inns & Pubs)	£3.50
Midlands (Inns & Pubs)	£3.50
West Country (Inns & Pubs)	£3.50
South East (Inns & Pubs)	£3.50
Your Garden in East Anglia	£4.00

Prices include postage and packing.

No order will be accepted without prior payment, other than from book retailers.

Recently Published.....

An original and informative guide to public gardens, garden centres and traders in Norfolk, Suffolk and Cambridgeshire.

Tips from the region's top growers and suppliers on roses, bonsai, conservatories, swimming pools, barbecues, aquatics, lawn care, landscaping and much more.

Over 100 colour photographs, including some of the most beautiful gardens.

Just £3.40 from most bookshops and some garden centres.

THE OLIVER TWIST

High Road, Guyhirn, nr Wisbech.   Tel. (0945) 75523
    Location: On A47, near Guyhirn Bridge.
    Credit cards: Access, Visa, Amex.
        Bitters: Tanglefoot, Marstons Pedigree, Greene King Abbott, Ruddles,
            plus two guests.
        Lagers: Red Stripe, Hansa, Carlsberg.

Examples of bar meals (lunch & evening, 7 days): *steaks with choice of sauce, chicken in orange sauce, rainbow trout with almonds, Dover sole bonne femme, seafood platter, Scottish salmon with prawn & parsley sauce, 20 chef's specialities.*
Examples of restaurant meals (lunch & evening, Tues - Sat): *duck in cherry sauce, steak Diane, seafood mornay, sole with prawn sauce, half chicken a la creme, beef stroganoff. Trad. Sun. roasts.*

Unlike the eponymous Dickens' hero, you will not need to ask for more after eating (the portions are ample), but with such a wide and exotic choice before you, you may be tempted to try more than one homecooked dish! In a range of over 30, you will find Italian, French, Chinese, Indian and of course English and others - an oasis of good food in the heart of Fenland, not an area noted for adventurous or cosmopolitan cuisine. At over 200 years, the pub is much older than first appears, and was a coaching inn. Inside is warm and hospitable, and the open brick fireplaces and timbered walls and ceilings confirm its antiquity. Barbecues are held occasionally in the patio garden, and children and small dogs are also permitted inside. Being right on the banks of the river Nene, there's good fishing to be had. Car park.

YE OLDE WHITE HART

Main Street, Ufford.   Tel. (0780) 740250
      Location: Edge of village.
      Credit cards: Not accepted.
      Bitters: Home Brewery, Theakstons Best, Old Peculier, SB, Youngers
                  Scotch and No. 3.
      Lagers: Becks, McEwans.

Examples of bar meals (lunchtime only, not Sundays or Mondays): *homemade pies, moussaka, steak & onions, fillet steak stuffed with stilton in port & herb sauce, ploughman's, sandwiches, daily specials. Children's choice. 3 course Sun. lunches (including 'beefy boats' filled Yorkshire puddings).*
Examples of a la carte (lunch & evening, except Sun. & Mon.): *'cor blimey' steak, saute of beef a la White Hart, Hooty's hearty mixed grill, jumbo prawns in garlic, veg. specials eg 'fake steak' au poivre, mushroom & asparagus hotpot, daily specials. Spotted dick, sloshed chocolate.*

On the only hill around, this 17th-century inn affords a stunning panorama of the exquisite honeystone village of Ufford and beyond. In good weather barbecues are held both at lunchtime and evening in the large garden, where children have a play area (they also have an acre of meadow), and will love the five cats, two goats, the dog and Boris the stuffed tarantula in the bar. The interior is pretty without being twee, with a log fire and a new snug. Landlord Chris Hooton is a qualified chef and wine expert. He holds theme evenings two or three times per year, and on alternate Sunday lunchtimes there's the novelty of live jazz to accompany the roast! Live folk music may be heard every Sunday evening. Wife Sally is particularly proud of the posh ladies' room, but not all readers will be able to enjoy this! Recommended by national guides. Large car park.

THE BELL INN

Great North Road, Stilton. Tel. (0733) 241066

Location: Village centre.
Credit cards: Access, Visa, Diners, Amex.
Accommodation: 2 singles, 14 doubles, 2 twins, 1 family, all en suite, with tea & coffee, satellite tv, 2 4-posters, 5 whirlpool baths. From £57 single. E.T.B. 4 Crowns Highly Commended, AA 3-Star.
Bitters: Marstons, Ruddles, Tetley, Theakstons, guests.
Lagers: Lowenbrau, Carlsberg.

Examples of bar meals (lunch & evening, 7 days): *Normandy soup, cajun prawns, steaks, Bell beef pie, baguettes, stilton & plum bread.*
Examples of restaurant meals (available as above): *timbale of prawn & crab mousse wrapped in Scotch smoked salmon, thin slices of smoked duck breast with fresh basil; Byron's fillet of beef, Bell chicken supreme, lavender lamb, trio of vegetarian filo parcels. Orange & Grand Marnier pancakes.*

Stilton is ofcourse one of the world's great cheeses, and it was an 18th century landlord of the Bell, Cooper Thornhill, who first popularised it - just a chapter in the story of one of England's historic inns. Dick Turpin evaded the law here and Cromwell, Byron, Clark Gable and Joe Louis have also propped up the bar in their time. A striking building inside and out, it was, no surprise, a coaching inn, and now that the village has been bypassed the old great road is eerily quiet - good news for overnight guests (some rooms overlook the courtyard and garden). Those not so keen on a restful night's sleep should ask for the old haunted bedroom! Naturally, stilton features prominently on the menus, and the home cooking has earned distinction in Egon Ronay and other major guides. Two function rooms. Backgammon available in the Village Bar.

THE CROSS KEYS HOTEL

16 Market Hill, Chatteris. Tel. (0354 69) 3036/2644
Location: Main Street, opposite church.
Credit cards: Access, Visa, Amex, Diners.
Accommodation: 7 twin/double rooms, most en suite, full facilities.
Tourist Board 3 crowns, RAC *, AA *.
Bitters: Greene King Abbbot, I.P.A.
Lagers: Harp.

Examples of bar meals (lunch & evening, 7 days): *mixed grill, fresh river trout stuffed with prawns & asparagus, homemade steak pie in real ale, sandwiches, omelettes, ploughmans.*
Examples of restaurant meals (lunchtime & evenings, 7 days): *steaks (speciality), Nobleman's Repast, Innkeeper's Pride, Traveller's Gift, Shepherd's Delight. Table d'hote, Sunday lunch.*

A 16th-century coaching inn, The Cross Keys retains much of its period character. The oak beamed bars are distinguished by antique clocks, rifles, and crackling log fires. The food is varied but invariably home cooking orientated, the mellow atmosphere an aid to digestion. The high standard of catering is available both on and off the premises for any private functions or small conferences. Children are welcome and are provided with a small play area in the garden. Richard and Sandra Skeggs have refurbished the bedrooms in excellent taste, with both charm and comfort in mind. One, The Cornwell Room, has a four-poster and is much in demand, and the hotel would make an ideal base for those wishing to visit Cambridge, Ely, Peterborough or King's Lynn.

YE OLDE FERRY BOAT INN

Holywell, nr St Ives.   Tel. (0480) 463227

        Location: River front, Gt River Ouse.

   Credit cards: Access, Visa.

Accommodation: 7 doubles, 1 twin, all with private facilities, 2 with 4-posters. From £39.99 incl.

        Bitters: Adnams Best & Broadside, Greene King, Fullers London Pride, Worthington, guest.

        Lagers: Carling, Tennents, Warsteiner.

Examples of bar meals (lunch & evening, 7 days): *tipple pie, salmon, curries, steaks, vegetarian dishes, daily specials, weekend extra specials. Homemade desserts. Barbecues in summer, weather permitting. Special evenings - ask for list of forthcoming events.*

A contender for the title 'England's oldest inn', the 'Ferryboat' is over 1,000 years old, preceding William the Conqueror by a century. One can only be a awestruck by such staggering antiquity. Parts of the original building still stand, in particular a rare fireplace with a window in it. As one might expect, a ghost is said to walk; the sad and harmless spirit of Juliette Tewsley, who hanged herself over unrequited love a millenium ago. Her gravestone forms part of the floor near the open fireplace, and she has a lovely spot in which to spend the rest of eternity. The timbered bar commands fine views over the large garden to the river, a marvellous backdrop for a wedding reception or party. There is a function room if weather precludes. Richard and Shelley Jeffrey are the owners, Hilary Paddock the manageress.

THE TRINITY FOOT

Huntingdon Road, Swavesey.   Tel. (0954) 30315
    Location: A604 Eastbound, 7 miles west of Cambridge.
  Credit cards: Access, Visa, Mastercard.
     Bitters: Flowers, Wethereds, Whitbreads.
     Lagers: Stella Artois, Heineken.

Examples of bar meals (lunchtime 7 days, every evening except Sunday): *fresh fish at most times, hot garlic prawns, smoked mackerkel, omelettes, ploughmans, trout, steaks, scampi, mixed grill, beef curry, salads. Sherry trifle, meringues glace, banana split, peach melba. Seasonal daily specials eg samphire, lobster, crab, oysters.*

Seafood is much more in evidence since the pub acquired its own fish shop, supplied from Lowestoft, Humberside and Loch Fyne. Also unusual, unique in fact, is the name Trinity Foot, after a pack of beagle hounds mastered by Colonel Whitbread, whose family's beer is on sale here. The hunters eschewed the usual fox as quarry, preferring hares, sportingly pursued on foot. The Trinity part of course refers to the nearby university college. John and Brenda Mole will serve you delicious freshly prepared food in portions to satisfy the most ardent trencherman, with special evenings like French, Spanish or Potuguese to add a little zest. Well-behaved children are welcome in the eating area or unleashed onto the large, safe lawn. A new conservatory has just been added, and planning consent is awaited for a marquee. Despite its proximity to the A604, traffic is high up on an embankment and is not over intrusive. Large car park. Featured in national good pub guides.

THE TRAVELLER'S REST

Ely Road, Chittering.   Tel. (0223) 860751

Location:	On A10 mid-way between Cambridge and Ely.
Credit cards:	Access, Visa.
Accommodation:	Caravan site adjacent.
Bitters:	Tolly Original, Tetley, guests.
Lagers:	Castelemaine, Stella Artois.

Examples of bar meals (lunch & evening, 7 days): *steak & kidney pie, Mexican dishes, cider baked pork, roast, curry, lasagne, fresh fish, scampi, traveller's lunch, many salads, daily specials. Children's menu.*
Examples of restaurant meals (as above): *lime & tarragon baked chicken with prawn & mushroom sauce, steaks, braised vension with juniper & cherry sauce, Dover sole stuffed with prawns & grilled in cheese sauce, nut loaf with apricot sauce. Carvery Fri & Sat (or for midweek parties of 15). Trad. Sun. roasts (booking advised).*

Keith and Sandy Richardson liked their local so much they bought it! That was some three years ago; Keith was a farm manager, Sandy in outside catering for 10 years. Their experience is reflected by the quality and variety of the food. Fresh vegetables and herbs are grown in their own two-acre garden; indeed, vegetarians and the health-conscious are especially well looked after. The main building is around 300 years old and was a halt for wagoners. They would have drawn water from the well in what is now a caravan site, and legend has it that many years ago a man fell in, his body never to be recovered. Occasional live music. Children welcome, and large garden has petanque (public playground to rear). Wickham Fen and Anglesea Abbey nearby.

THE CARPENTER'S ARMS

76 Brook Street, Soham.   Tel. (0353) 720869

      Location: Turn off main road opp. Cherry Tree pub.

Credit cards: Not accepted.

        Bitters: Batemans, Marston's Pedigree, Old Speckled Hen, Everard's Tiger, Thwaites, Varsity, Wadworth 6X, Adnams, Greene King Abbot, Old Hook Norton.

        Lagers: Kronenbourg, Tennents, Carling.

Examples of bar meals (11am - 11pm Mon - Sat, 12 - 2pm Sun): *moussaka, chilli, lasagne, curry (Sats), burgers, liver & bacon, scampi, plaice, cod, haddock, salads, ploughman's, sandwiches, roast (Sats)*.

One of the best selections of choicest ales in the region makes this 18th century pub a must for all serious beer drinkers, and it is no surprise that it is recommended by CAMRA. It would also appear to be the focus of social life hereabouts: the local football team refresh themselves in the single large bar after a game (their trophies are displayed over the fireplace), an angling club meets, quiz nights and monthly live music are popular attrcations, and there are no less than three pool and five darts teams - landlord Allan Killick was himself a county player. Whatever your reason for a visit, he and wife Jenny, who took over five years ago, extend a cordial greeting, children included. The many prints of aeroplanes decorating the walls will interest some readers. Function room for up to 50. New patio and garden.

THE THREE BLACKBIRDS

Woodditton, nr Newmarket.   Tel. (0638) 730811
      Location: Village centre.
 Credit cards: Access, Visa.
       Bitters: Greene King, Tetley. Plus Guinness, dry Blackthorn cider.
       Lagers: Castlemaine, Stella Artois, plus large range of bottled.

Examples of bar/restaurant meals (lunch & evening, 7 days): *stuffed mushrooms, white asparagus, calamares, seafood gratin, venison in red wine, chicken in white wine & grain mustard & cream sauce, Scotch steaks, scampi, plaice, haddock, breadcrumbed escalope of pork in provencal sauce, lasagne (noted), homecooked ham, fish specialities (noted), vegetarian dish of the day, blackboard specials. Trad. Sun. lunch.*

A huge collection of business cards (including that of a High Commissioner of New Zealand) from all over the world, pinned around the bar, is eloquent testimony to the wide renown of this thatched and beamed 17th-century village pub, regularly feted by the major national guides. Credit for this must go to proprietors Joan and Ted Spooner, who came here 12 years ago from a restaurant in Spain. Being so close to Newmarket, much of the clientele is from the world of racing, including some famous faces, but the reception from both sides of the bar is always friendly, and this 'spirit' is also entered into apparently by the ghost of a victim murdered here 300 years ago! Pride is taken in the fresh, homecooked food, which may be enjoyed in the bar or restaurant. Well behaved children are welcome, and the garden has a play area. Well placed for Cambridge and most parts of the region.

THE THREE HILLS

Bartlow, nr Linton.   Tel. (0223) 891259
   Location: One mile off A604 Cambridge-Haverhill Road.
Credit cards: Access, Visa, Mastercard.
    Bitters: Greene King.
     Lagers: Kronenbourg.

Examples of bar meals (lunch & evening, 7 days): *trout in almonds, fine Scotch steaks, turbot, monkfish (grills & fresh fish a speciality), lamb cutlets, gammon grilled with fresh pineapple, vegetarian (only fresh local produce used, when possible). Banana tropic, selection of speciality luxury icecreams, homeade syllabub & pavlova.*
Examples of restaurant meals (as above): *similar to bar meals but far more extensive, and may be enjoyed in comfort of dining room.*

A visit to The Three Hills will confirm that our better pubs have much to offer. Here good English and international fare is presented by hosts Sue and Steve Dixon, prepared with care and served generously, earning a place in most leading guides. Their attractive 15th century inn has the interior of the quintessential English pub - oak beams blending with polished brasswork and inglenooks, logs burning within when needed. Children are welcome in the restaurant and also in the very pleasant walled garden. The surrounds are idyllic, perhaps because of being somewhat off the well trodden path, and juke boxes and other agents of deafness do not spoil the tranquillity. The hills referred to are Roman burial mounds, of great interest to antiquarians. Car parking.

THE JOHN BARLEYCORN

Moorfield Road, Duxford. Tel. (0223) 832699
Location: Village centre.
Credit cards: Not accepted.
Bitters: Greene King.
Lagers: Kronenbourg, Harp.

Examples of bar meals (lunch & evening, 7 days, except Christmas day): *smoked haddock with poached eggs, homemade salmon mousse, casseroled pigeon, lamb & vegetable pie, open salad sandwiches. Grills include sirloin, trout, gammon. Homemade sweets.*

If you wanted to show a foreign guest the ideal English country pub, then you need look no further than the John Barleycorn. The name itself belongs to ancient folklore; celebrated in song it is a kind of shorthand for the natural things that make up good ale. Find yourself a corner in the single, snug bar and sample some of the delicious and very original fare, which has earned enthusiastic reviews in national guides and local journals. Or take to the pleasant garden at the rear where a small barn has been converted to the Garden Room. Barbecues are held here, and you may arrange your own party (min. 10 people). Christmas starts on December 1st, from when an extensive special menu becomes effective. Book early to see in the New Year with a supper party, followed by some fancy footwork on the dance floor, perhaps!

THE WHITE HORSE

Great North Road, Eaton Socon.   Tel. (0480) 474453
        Location: Village centre - Main road.
    Credit cards: Mastercard, Visa.
 Accommodation: Three doubles. £37.50 single, £40 double B & B.
         Bitters: Flowers Original, Boddingtons, Wethereds, Whitbread Best,
                  Poacher.
         Lagers: Stella Artois, Heineken.

Examples of bar meals (lunch & evening, 7 days): *steak pie, chicken Kiev, lasagne, chilli, steaks, cod, plaice, salads, ploughman's.*
Examples of restaurant meals (lunch & evening Tues - Sat, plus trad. Sun. lunch): *salmon roti, panfried venison in rich sauce with juniper berries, breast of chicken (with homemade stuffing) served with hazelnut liqueur sauce.*

Dickens and Pepys were but two of many to rest at this former coaching inn on the Great North Road, situated near the River Ouse. Inside, history impresses itself on the visitor. The rooms are cosy with high back settles and with a superb inglenook housing a cheering log fire. The tables are topped with warm copper and its natural counterpart, brass, shines from horse brasses and platters. The new proprietors continue to offer extensive menus, accompanied by a wine list well above the norm, and the quality earns places in major national guides. A friendly lady ghost is said to visit, obviously temporarily forsaking paradise to be here. Large beer garden with children's play area.

16

THE BELL

Horsefair Lane, Odell. Tel. (0234) 720254
Location: Village centre.
Credit cards: Not acceped.
Bitters: Greene King.
Lagers: Harp, Kronenbourg.

Examples of bar meals (no cooked food on Sundays): *homemade pies (eg turkey with leek & mushroom, or pork with apple & cider, or steak & kidney), meat platters, scampi, roast chicken, gammon steak, pizzas, vegetable flan, bacon flan, sandwiches, ploughman's, blackboard specials. Torte Montmarte, cheesecake, chocolate fudge gateau.*

It looks every inch the ideal thatched country pub, and for once appearances are not deceptive. Tucked away in a quiet village, not far from Odell Country Park, its 16th century origins are apparent from the superb inglenook and exposed beams in the five rather cosy bar areas. One may eat anywhere and be sure of good, home-produced food, prepared by the landlady herself, Doreen Scott (look for the blackboard specials). With husband Derek she has been at The Bell for about seven years, and they have made it popular for the friendly atmosphere, (no wailing jukeboxes to disturb), as much as the good food. Children have an area set aside for them, but will be sure to head for the little river which tumbles past at the end of the garden. Not one to be missed, and rated by major national guides.

THE MAD DOG

Little Odell.   Tel. (0234) 720221

      Location: On Harrold to Sharnbrook road.
Credit cards: Access, Visa.
       Bitters: Greene King.
       Lagers: Harp, Kronenbourg.

Examples of lunchtime bar meals (7 days): *homemade steak & kidney pie, chicken & mushroom pie, chilli, cod, plaice, king rib, steakwich, sandwiches, ploughman's, jacket potatoes, daily specials, vegetarian menu eg spinach & cheese cannaloni, veg. curry. Apple strudel, sponge pudding, gateau.*

Examples of evening bar meals (7 days): *as above plus:- chicken breast stuffed with leeks & served in stilton sauce, local venison (speciality), scampi, curry, steak, gammon, lamb chop, specials.*

"The little pub with the large menu" - a fair summary of this attractive 16th century stone and thatch hostelry. But there's much more to say about it: the odd name derives from the original landlord, who is said to have dispensed treatment for dogbites. Maybe it is one of his hapless patients who has been the cause of mysterious happenings, reported by generations of landlords, particularly in the room with the inglenook. The interesting decor includes a collection of scales, gin traps, china plates, and a rare poster with the legend "Help the war effort. Drink draught beer". Proprietors (for 10 years) Ken and Jean Parry organise occasional midweek barbecues, and theme evenings in winter. Children are welcome in the garden where there's a special play area with an old circus roundabout, swings and Wendy House. In CAMRA good beer guide for last eight years.

THE ROSE & CROWN

69 High Street, Ashwell, nr Baldock.   Tel. (0462 74) 2420
      Location: Village centre.
   Credit cards: Visa, Mastercard, Eurocard.
      Bitters: Greene King.
      Lagers: Harp, Kronenbourg.

Examples from lunchtime menu (Tues - Sun): *peppered goat's cheese on toasted French bread, Crown smokies, homebaked ham, steak & kidney pie with Abbot ale, salmon & broccoli pie, steaks, jacket potatoes, sandwiches, daily special. Trad. Sun. roasts.*
Examples from evening menu (Tues - Sun): *lemon sole fillet with orange sauce, medallions of English lamb (sauted in wine, garlic & rosemary), half pheasant in whisky sauce, seafood collage in light creamy sauce, steaks, mushroom stroganoff, vegetable au gratin, seasonal specials.*
NB Tuesday is "fish & chip day", lunch & evening.

We all know of pubs that have been spoiled by too much emphasis on food: one feels guilty in just asking for a drink. Whilst quality homecooked food - varied regularly - is very important here, one may equally enjoy a relaxed, unhurried drink in an amiable atmosphere, without feeling under any obligation to eat. The bar is divided into four cosy areas, one set aside for games. Courting couples should look for the 'nooky seat'. The magnificent inglenook indicates great age, and the building is said to be haunted, not unusual in a 15th century coaching inn. Children are welcome in eating areas or in the very pleasant garden to the rear of the car park.

THE LYTTON ARMS

Park Lane, Knebworth.   Tel. (0438) 812312
     Location: Mid-way between Knebworth & Codicote.
  Credit cards: Access, Visa.
       Bitters: Shefford, Adnams, Bass, Theakstons, 6 guests.
       Lagers: Becks, Carslberg, plus imported bottled. Range of real
              ciders from the cellar.

Examples of bar meals (lunch & evening, 7 days): *stilton mushrooms, deep fried brie, steaks, mixed grill, chicken Kiev, homemade steak & mushroom pie, trout with prawns, chicken tikka, homemade lasagne, scampi, cod, quiche, salads, ploughman's, sandwiches, daily specials. Cheesecake, spotted dick, lemon meringue pie.*

Knebworth House is one of the most noteworthy stately homes in the land, and this traditional 19th-century country pub is part of the Lytton family estate (old photographs of the Lyttons and Knebworth form part of the decor in the lounge bar). So the countryside in these parts is very pleasant, ideal for ramblers and cyclists, and after stretching the legs and filling the lungs you'll be ready for a good beer and wholesome home-prepared food. Both are available in good measure here (and a log fire in winter), and the wide range of 'real' ales has earned a place in the Camra guide. Proprietor Stephen Nye has been pulling pints here for about five years. There's a garden and patio (barbecues summer weekends) with play facilities for children, and large car park.

THE GEORGE & DRAGON

High Street, Watton-at-Stone. Tel. (0920) 830285
Location: Village centre, between Stevenage & Hertford.
Credit cards: Access, Visa, Diners, Amex.
Bitters: Greene King. Plus draught Guinness & dry Blackthorn cider.
Lagers: Harp, Kronenbourg.

Examples of bar meals (lunch & evening, except Sunday evenings): *Corsican fish soup, tomato & basil tart, 'millionaire's bun' (with fillet steak), lambs' kidneys in madeira wine, strips of pork fillet cooked in sauce (with bean shoots, ginger & spring onions), vegetarian dish, salads, sandwiches, ploughman's, dish of the day.*
Examples of restaurant meals (lunch & evening, except Sunday evenings): *Alsatian hot savoury onion tart, herring roes in butter & fresh lime, paupiettes of fresh sole filled with salmon mousse, chicken breast stuffed with black cherries & covered with white wine & dill sauce, steaks, pimento filled with spiced kidney bean bordelaise.*

"The pub with the club atmosphere" - that's how it's often known, the achievement over the years of Kevin and Christine Dinnin. Not only the warmth and hospitality are outstanding: the homecooked food, as a glance over the examples above will suggest, is of the first order, sufficient to secure a regular place, indeed a star rating, in the main national pub guides. Occasional special nights add further interest, and the wine list is always excellent. Built as a pub in 1603, it exudes an air of comfort and well being, with its old beams, antique furniture and prints, and fresh flowers in abundance. To relax by the log fire with the papers (provided) and good food and drink is a simple pleasure not to be missed. Children welcome as far as facilities will allow, but there is a garden and patio.

THE ROSE & CROWN

41 Upper Green Road, Tewin, nr Welwyn.   Tel. (0438) 717257
   Location: Just off B1000, 3) miles from juncion 6 of A1.
   Credit cards: Access, Visa.
   Bitters: Greene King. Double X dark mild.
   Lagers: Kronenbourg, Harp, Harp Premier.

Examples from lunchtime menu (Mon - Sat): *roast beef, steak & mushroom pie, Abbot ale pie, savoury mince & dumplings, lasagne, chilli, 'Crowner' double decker sandwich, ploughman's, vegetarian selection. Trad. Sun. roast.*
Examples from evening menu (not Sundays): *steaks, scampi, plaice, chicken Kiev, mixed grill, garlic chicken, nut fetuccini.*

A favourite English pastime is a spin in the country to find a traditional country pub. The Rose & Crown is just such a one, standing by a village green in pleasant countryside. Dating from around 1650, it was part of a farm, and from 1738 it was the meeting place of the first Hertfordshire Friendly Societies. It was also obviously favoured by poachers, for the box where they hid their game can still be seen in one of the two spacious bars. Comfortable seating, soft lighting and a roaring fire are conducive to good digestion, and one may eat anywhere at lunchtime, but in the evening food is served by waiters in the dining room, which can double as a function room. Halloween, Valentine, St George and other red-letter days are faithfully observed, and in summer barbecues are held in the garden (with play area). Children welcome under supervision. Near trout farm, Stanborough Lakes and Roman Baths.

THE FOX & HOUNDS

High Street, Hunsdon. Tel. (0279) 842369
Location: Village centre.
Credit cards: Access, Visa, Mastercard, Eurocard.
Bitters: Greene King Abbot & IPA, Rayments.
Lagers: Stella Artois, Kronenbourg, Harp.

Examples of bar meals (lunch & evening, 7 days): *mushroom & tarragon soup, chicken breast with Cumberland sauce, homemade steak & kidney pie, crispy roast duck with orange sauce, prime plaice fillet, vegetarian dishes, ploughman's, sandwiches. Menu revised daily.*
Examples of restaurant meals (as above): *avocado filled with crab & baked in rich cheese & wine sauce, rack of lamb with apricot stuffing & lamb jus, braised saddle of venison (in cognac, port & cranberries), poached sea bream with saffron sauce, sirloin steak. Trad Sun roast £9 (3 courses).*

Carl Yardley trained as a chef at London's Hilton Hotel, so expect far-above-average pub fare when you come to this peaceful, pretty little village, just minutes from Harlow. He and wife Pauline completely overhauled their attractive 17th-century pub when they took over in 1990. The best of English pub traditions live on: large open fireplaces, beams and studwork, horse bits and brasses, and decor on the theme of fox, hounds and horses. Traditional celebrations are also honoured, such as Valentine and Beaujolais nights. Children are especially welcome; smaller portions are available, and there are outdoor games (including bouncy castle) and a barbecue in the garden. Dining room also available for functions.

THE WHITE HART

High Street, Puckeridge, nr Ware. Tel. (0920) 821309
Location: Junction of A10 with A120.
Credit cards: Access, Visa, Diners.
Bitters: McMullens Country, AK, Courage Directors, Abbot.
Lagers: Stella Artois, Fosters, Steingold.

Examples of bar/restaurant meals (lunch & evening, 7 days): *hot Arbroath smokie with cheese, rollmop herring stuffed with prawns, pastrami, chicken sate with peanut butter sauce, steaks, homemade turkey & mushroom pie, moussaka, lasagne, lobster, poached halibut steak with seafood sauce, large vegetarian menu, daily roast, ploughman's, sandwiches. Children's menu. Senior citizen's special lunch £3.50 (3 courses + coffee) every Thursday.*

Will you take up the 'seafood platter salad challenge'? If you can completely consume (unaided) a huge plateful of cold seafood with salad, you will be presented with a voucher for £6.95 to be deducted from your next meal. It's a bold offer from affable hosts Colin and Rita Boom, who've been here 12 years, and whose speciality is seafood - they've just wone the Seafood Pub of the Year Award. But there's much else to commend at this celebrated lovely old Tudor pub, star-rated by good food guides and the Vegetarian Society Handbook. Colin follows in the distinguished footsteps of Henry VIII and the Duke of Wellington in acquiring the manorship of Standon Rectory, mentioned in Domesday. Over 5's are welcome, and will thrill to the Shetland ponies, sheep, ducks, rabbits etc, and swings in the garden. Ask about the odd tale of 'the lady up the chimney'.

THE YEW TREE INN

36 The Street, Manuden, nr Bishops Stortford.
Tel. (0279) 812888

Location: 10 mins from Stansted Airport.
Credit cards: Access, Visa, Eurocard.
Accommodation: 1 single, 4 doubles, 1 family, all en suite.
Bitters: Flowers IPA, Greene King Abbot, Theakstons.
Lagers: Stella Artois, Heineken, Heineken Export.

Examples of bar meals (lunch & evening, except Sun. evening): *homemade steak & kidney pie, chilli, lasagne, chicken ham & mushroom pie, steaks, salads, ploughman's, sandwiches, daily specials eg Japanese prawns, beef stroganoff.*
Examples of restaurant meals (every evening except Sun.): *trout with almonds, steaks, mixed grill.*

The Yew Tree and Manuden have been acquainted for 550 years, and together represent the best of English traditions. A very pretty village in one of the most unspoilt corners of Essex, yet not far from Stansted Airport, it makes an ideal base for an overnight stay (bedrooms are well appointed). The many period features are further beautified by lovely floral displays, at which landlady Jacqui Kinnison excels. Also worth a special note is the exceptionally well kept IPA, which "drinks like wine". A recent addition is a super new restaurant, carefully constructed from ships' timbers to blend with the established building. English, continental and vegetarian cuisine, with stress on freshness, enjoy a a fine reputation. Functions of all kinds, including conferences, are catered for, but the romantic atmosphere lends itself to wedding receptions, a speciality.

THE AXE AND COMPASSES

Arkesden, nr Saffron Walden.   Tel. (0799) 550272
Location: Village centre.
Credit cards: Access, Visa.
Bitters: Greene King IPA & Abbot, Rayments Special.
Lagers: Kronenbourg, Harp.

Examples of bar meals (lunch & evening, except Sun evening): *homemade steak & kidney pie, lamb cutlets, sirloin steak, chicken chasseur, lasagne, moules mariniere, skate, king prawns, cod, plaice, sandwiches, ploughman's.*
Examples of restaurant meals (as above): *pan-fried chicken supreme with port & stilton sauce, roast duck breast, peppered sirloin, tenderloin of pork, grilled whole lemon sole, poached salmon, vegetables in filo pastry with tangy sauce, vegetable stroganoff. Trad. Sun. roasts.*
NB Children eat at half price.

Newcomers to Arkesden wonder why they've never heard of it before. It is, quite simply, exquisite, and puts many a more famous place to shame. Grand old thatched houses straddle a little stream in the dappled shade of willow trees. For complete perfection a lovely old country pub is required, and that's what you have in 'The Axe and Compasses' - a picturebook 17th- century house, presided over since October 1992 by new owner Themis Christou and family. Many readers will know of Themis from his 12 very successful years at the Coach and Horses, Trumpington (near Cambridge).

The menus, revised regularly, blend time-honoured English favourites such as steak and kidney pie or roast duck breast with equally venerated French dishes like moules mariniere and chicken chasseur, together with imaginative vegetarian cooking, acknowledging a modern trend. Likewise, fresh fish is always featured.

Star rating in national good pub guide. Children welcome in restaurant and patio areas. Definitely not one to be missed!

Axe & Compasses, Arkesden

THE CROWN

Little Walden, nr Saffron Walden.
Location: 1¹/₂ miles north of Saffron Walden.
Credit cards: Access, Visa, Mastercard, Eurocard.
Bitters: Boddingtons, Greene King IPA, everchanging guests.
Lagers: Stella Artois, Heineken. Good range of bottles.

Tel. (0799) 522475

Examples of bar meals (lunch & evening, except Sun. evening): *baked mackerel, kidneys turbigo, steak & kidney pie, steaks, chilli, jugged hare with buttered noodles, liver & bacon, escalope of pork cordon bleu, curry, smoked seafood platter, whole plaice, wild mushroom stroganoff, jacket potatoes, daily specials eg skate, mussels in garlic, seafood quiche. Menu revised daily. Trad. Sun. roasts.*

National winner of Egon Ronay's "Pub of the Year" in the recent past, this is obviously no ordinary establishment. The stimulating menu, blending the new and traditional (from the kitchen of new chef Chris Page), is chalked daily on a blackboard. Likewise, the bitters are changed regularly, and mostly served straight from the barrel. Unchanging, however, is the building itself, once two 18th century cottages, although the low doors, walk-through fireplaces and timber lattices suggest much older origins, especially in the 'snug' (children welcome). Flooring ranges from terra cotta to stripped wood via luxury pile carpet, furniture is solid wood and there's a fine old grandfather clock in one corner. Steve and Sue are a friendly young couple who came here only in summer '91, and who like to celebrate New Year in style, plus other red letter days like Valentine, Halloween etc.

THE PRINCE OF WALES

Brick End, Broxted.

Tel. (0279) 850256
Fax (0279) 874516

Location: Village centre.
Credit cards: Access, Visa, Amex.
Bitters: Ruddles, Websters.
Lagers: Holsten, Fosters, Kaliber.

Examples of bar/restaurant meals (lunch & evening, 7 days): *steak kidney & Guinness cobbler, chicken supreme with bacon & field mushrooms, pigeon breasts en croute on rich game sauce, rack of lamb with mint & almond sauce, pan-fried sand soles with lemon, poached fillet of plaice with crab & prawns, steaks, homemade pies, vegetarian dishes (eg spinach, mushroom & cream cheese roulade). Bread & butter pudding, summer fruit crumble, Florentine cream cake, chocolate zuccotto. Trad. Sun. roasts (booking advised).*
NB Chef's policy is to dispense with a set menu and instead feature on the chalkboard in each dining area a frequently changing selection based on the freshest daily ingredients.

Already one of the leading pubs in this lovely corner of Essex, recent additions have made The Prince of Wales a must for any visitor to the area. Foremost among these are a large new conservatory overlooking a new enclosed children's log play area, and an attractive terrace with hanging baskets and barrels planted up. The menu, far superior to average pub fare, may be enjoyed in either bar, restaurant or conservatory - prices are the same. The homely main bar is furnished cottage-style, and the partly beamed walls are bedecked with old photos showing Broxted village life and people. The pub has been 15 years in the same family ownership.

THE THREE HORSESHOES

Mole Hill Green, Takeley, nr Bishops Stortford.   Tel. (0279) 870313
Location: Edge of village, nr Stansted Airport.
Credit cards: Visa.
Bitters: Benskins, Adnams, occasional guest.
Lagers: Lowenbrau, Castlemaine, Skol, Swan Light.

Examples of bar meals (lunch & evening, 7 days): *vlammetjes (spicy spring rolls), chicken fingers with honey mustard dip, poached salmon with hollandaise sauce, steaks, spinach & mushroom lasagne, huffers, salads, ploughman's, sandwiches, daily specials. Lemon mousse, Mississippi mud pie, Dutch apple pie. Trad. Sun. roasts (booking advised).*

Stansted airport continues to grow in importance, but the surrounding villages, many of them very pretty, slumber on apparently unconcerned. One such is Mole Hill Green, further blessed with his striking 400-year-old country pub. Michael and Lynn Tarrant are the well-travelled proprietors. Michael is a pilot, which explains the aviation memorabilia and collection of foreign currency amongst the low beams, log fire and oak settles. They have also brought back with them a number of exotic dishes, adding a little spice to the traditional English fare. For extra stimulation look out for special theme evenings, as well as quiz nights and occasional live jazz in summer. Indoor pusuits include backgammon, and in the lovely garden are to be found swings, a slide, barbecue and duck pond. Children are permitted inside if eating with adults. Caravan parking at rear.

THE BUTCHER'S ARMS

Dunmow Road, North End, Gt Dunmow. Tel. (0245) 37481
Location: On A130.
Credit cards: Mastercard, Visa.
Bitters: Ridley's IPA, McEwans.
Lagers: Fosters, Holsten, Carlsberg Export.

Examples of bar meals (every lunchtime, evenings except Sun): *steaks, chicken Kiev, scampi, haddock, lasagne verdi, chef's grill, spinach & mushroom lasagne, vegetable chilli, freshly made pizzas, ploughman's, huffers, sandwiches, daily specials. Apple & sultana sponge, spotted dick, chocolate icecream bomb. Children's meals. Trad. Sun. roasts from Oct. - Easter (booking advised).*

Monks from nearby Black Chapel built this as their 'local' back in 1459, and vistors were accommodated here. They did their work well, for the ancient oak beams are still bearing up, and look good for another 500 years. Mark and Jo Cracknell have established a cordial atmosphere and a reputation for good, straightforward food, very reasonably priced. Bookings are taken for tables in bar or restaurant area. Families are especially welcome (the pub features in 'Let's Go With the Children' guide), and youngsters will love the menagerie in the large garden, as well as swings and climbing frame. The adjacent one-acre meadow is available for use by registered caravan clubs, or indeed any society seeking an outdoor venue.

THE JOHN BARLEYCORN

Threshers Bush, High Laver, nr Old Harlow.   Tel. (0279) 422675
    Location: Gilden Way (off Churchgate Street).
  Credit cards: Access, Visa, Diners, Amex.
     Bitters: Eagle IPA, Courage Best, John Smiths, Websters.
     Lagers: Kronenbourg, Fosters, Carlton LA.

Examples from lunch menu (closed Monday lunch): *barbecue ribs, chicken satay, giant Yorkshire pudding filled with beans & sausages, local cured ham, Japanese prawn dip, deep fried breaded veggies, salads, ploughman's. Trad. Sun. roasts £9.95 (children £5.50), booking advised.*
Examples from evening restaurant menu (7:30 - 9pm, not Suns or Mons): *potato shells & chilli, stuffed garlic mushrooms, calamari; steaks, mountainous mixed grill, homemade steak & kidney pie, chicken tikka mosala, mixed fish grill, wild salmon tranche, vegetarian menu. Booking advised Thurs - Sat.*

Be prepared to loosen a button or two; portions are gigantic, the quality outstanding yet prices most affordable. John and Linda McHugh have won considerable renown over four years for their food but are conscious that this is first and foremost a pub. Dining is restricted to the candlelit restaurant in the evening, a delightful vaulted room in which coffins were once made! The timbered bar, too, is quite charming, also candlelit, with log fires, a Welsh dresser and an abundance of blue and white china. The award-winning garden with lily pond (and swings) is a joy to behold, and in season a stunning floral display covers the front of the 15th century building. Morris dancers add their colour on occasion. Well behaved children are welcome in the restaurant. Barbecues. Outside bar. Weddings etc a speciality.

THE BLACK BULL

Dunmow Road, Fyfield, nr Ongar.   Tel. (0277 899) 225

Location:	On B184 Ongar to Dunmow road.
Credit cards:	Access, Visa.
Bitters:	Wadworth 6X, Courage Best & Directors.
Lagers:	Fosters, Carlsberg, Kronenbourg.

Examples of bar meals (lunch & evening, 7 days): *flaked smoked haddock in cheese & wine sauce, field mushrooms in garlic butter, guacamole, Mediterranean prawns, chicken tikka with pitta bread, steaks. Fish night on Thursdays.*
Lunchtime only: *steak & kidney pie, chilli, jacket potatoes, variety of ploughmans, sandwiches.*

Now a freehouse, The Black Bull is widely regarded as being one of the best pubs for food in these parts. Proprietor Alan Smith has achieved this status by taking great pains to preserving high standards - deep frying is frowned on, and the menus are highly original, even exotic, and prepared with skill. Wild field mushrooms and a chilli that "takes no prisoners" are hardly typical pub fare. Fish lovers should be sure not to miss Thursday nights. It seems to have paid off, for the three bars always seem to be doing a good trade (indeed, an extension seating 28 has been added), and the large car park is a neccessity. The building is 600 years old - not immediately evident from the outside, but inside is rich with heavy timbers and open fires. The atmosphere is hospitable, the staff friendly and courteous. Children welcome in gardens.

THE ALMA ARMS

Horseman Side, Navestock Side, Brentwood.   Tel. (0277) 372629

Location:	3 miles off Brentwood/Ongar Road.
Credit Cards:	Not accepted.
Bitters:	Adnams, Greene King, Mauldons, Ridleys, Rayments.
Lagers:	Kronenbourg, Harp, Carlsberg.

Examples of bar meals (12 noon - 2 p.m. 7.00-8:45pm, 7 days): *homemade pies (eg steak, lasagne, shepherds, chicken), fresh daily fish (eg salmon, trout, lemon sole), seafood lasagne, grills & steaks (Saturdays). Homemade desserts (eg cheesecake, sherry trifle, fruit crumbles, bread & butter pudding). Daily 3 course meal £5.75 (Sat. menu £7.95) Trad. Sun. roasts (incl. dessert) £6.75.*

The Alma Arms is close to Brentwood and Harold Hill (A128) and the drive, once off the main road, through the Essex countryside is very pleasant, though not straightforward. Alan and Jane have run this busy rural inn for over 20 years, providing a varied homemade menu with the accent on value and freshness, complemented by a good range of ales. Please note the menu is extended on a Saturday night. The inn was built in 1731 but only bore the 'Alma' title since the Crimean War battle of that name. The attractive bars are oak beamed - the bar itself being brick with timber reliefs, the theme being continued to the fireplaces. A new addition is the very pleasant 40-seater Victorian conservatory, but for really warm days there is a patio to the front. Mentioned in several national guides. Large car park.

THE DUKE OF YORK

Southend Road, Billericay. Tel. (0277) 651403
Location: On A129 to Wickford (old Southend Road), 1 mile from town.
Credit cards: Access, Visa, Amex, Diners.
Bitters: Greene King Abbot & IPA, Rayments, McEwans, Toby.
Lagers: Heineken, Tennents, Tennents Extra, Kronenbourg, Red Stripe. Plus Strongbow & Red Rock ciders.

Examples of bar meals (lunch & evening every day except Sat. & Sun. evenings): *homemade soups & pies, salads, jacket potatoes with various fillings, steaks, curries, sandwiches, many daily specials eg spaghetti with prawns peppers & cream, bubble & squeak, pork chops Swiss style.*
Examples of restaurant meals (as above): *scallops mornay, steaks, Dover sole meuniere, veal georgette, large vegetarian menu (vegans catered for), many daily specials eg strips of chicken in potted shrimp sauce, monkfish in mussel & smoked salmon sauce, beef Wellington in red wine sauce. Trad. Sun. roasts £4.45.*

The Duke of York began life as two cottages (circa 1800), later in 1868 it became a beer house and in 1975 an extension in the form of a restaurant was added. The enthusiastic chef cooks to order from an enormous menu (in French and German also), yet achieves the distinction of a quality restaurant (expect to pay around £25 per head for a full meal) alongside a good pub at more everyday prices. Proprietor Mrs. Edna White dare not change things too much and risk incurring the displeasure of 'Swanee' - ghost in residence. Other spirits include over 50 malt whiskies, and the wine list has some real classics alongside the more modest. Children are permitted in the restaurant and everyone can bask on the small patio. Look for the antique cash till, in £ s d! Large car park.

THE HURDLE MAKERS ARMS

Post Office Road, Woodham Mortimer, nr Maldon.   Tel. (0245) 225169
- Location: Between A414 and B1010.
- Credit cards: Not accepted.
- Bitters: Greene King IPA & Abbott.
- Lagers: Heineken, Tennents Extra, Red Stripe.

Examples of bar meals (lunchtimes only, 7 days): *lasagne, Scotch smoked salmon salad, ham off the bone, homemade steak kidney & mushroom pie, Mediterranean prawn salad, various fillings in rolls & sandwiches, ploughmans, Devon smoked prawns, curries, smoked chicken, grilled lemon sole. Homemade fruit pie.*

Winner of the Camra 'Pub of the Year' (1988), The Hurdle Makers has a name and style all its own. It began life as a farmhouse, changed to an off-licence and, in 1871, finally became a pub. It is set in two acres of well tended garden, wherein is a children's play area - there's also a family room. Such a garden readily accommodates regular barbecues (and comprehensive salad bar) at which up to 200 can sit under 'sunbrellas', which can convert into a marquee if necessary. There's also a pitch-and-putt driving range to the rear, and the pub has its own golf society. The menu above, though typical, changes weekly. The food is totally fresh and never fried; Terry and Sue Green take pride in that, and also advise customers that no bookings are taken, just arrive. Inside you'll find two lovely oak beamed bars with stone flagged floors, settles dotted round tables and an open fire. All the washrooms are immaculate, and the disabled have their own. Pub bar has darts, dominoes and shut-the-box.

THE JOLLY SAILOR

Church Street, Hythe Quay, Maldon.   Tel. & Fax (0621) 853463
        Location: Quayside, bottom of Church Street.
    Credit Cards: Visa.
  Accommodation: 2 doubles, 2 twins.
          Bitters: Courage Directors, Ruddles, Websters, Trumans mild.
          Lagers: Kronenbourg, Fosters, Carlsberg.

Examples of bar meals (available all opening hours): *ploughmans, sandwiches, daily specials e.g. lamb cutlets, gammon steaks, fresh prawn salad, plaice, cod, sausage, French bread specials, vegetarain dishes. Evenings only: pizzas (specify toppings), steak meals.*

The Jolly Sailor is described by the D.O.E. as a "16th century timber framed house with 18th century plastered front. Commenced as public house in 1874". Such dry prose does not do justice to a fine quayside inn. Transforms from sailing barges are mounted on plaques forming a most attractive and unusual theme to the decor. Navigation lights from ships provide illumination to match, and the bar has the traditional oak beams. If you like a taste of the briney air with your drink, repair to the large attractive garden and patio overlooking the quay, and be serenaded by birdsong from the aviary. Lovely Maldon park and the town itself are close at hand, and as parking at the Jolly Sailor is limited this may be the best way to plan your visit. The food is wholesome, mostly homemade and very reasonably priced. In summer, Gordon and Phil Bell lay on a barbecue to which children are also welcome. Incidentally, the pub was featured in the TV series 'Lovejoy'.

THE GREEN DRAGON

Upper London Road, Young's End, nr Braintree.

Tel. (0245) 361030
Fax (0245) 362575

Location:	A131 2 miles south of Braintree - nr Essex showground.
Credit cards:	Visa, Mastercard, Amex, Luncheon vouchers.
Bitters:	Greene King Abbott, L.A. bottled selection.
Lagers:	Harp, Kronenbourg, Tennents LA.

Examples of bar meals (lunch & evening, 7 days): *homemade pies, Scotch salmon, trout, mussels, lasagne, salads, Indian style chicken, fresh crab, daily blackboard specials, vegetarian dishes.*

Examples of seasonal restaurant meals (as above): *baked avocado & spicy chicken topped with gruyere, sliced breast of local duckling with raspberry & port sauce, beefsteak kidney & mushroom pie, venison steak with onion sauce, steak Diane, Nile perch with beurre blanc & caviar, salmon supreme Mesquite, brown rice & hazelnut loaf with redcurrant & orange sauce. Revised regularly, and theme evenings include Greek, Beaujolais, Elizabethan etc.*

Catering awards and accolades are routinely visited upon The Green Dragon, to the credit of Bob and Mandy Greybrook. But the pub has been one of the best liked in the area for many years. The restaurant, which seats 46, was once the old stable block but is now ingeniously converted, even retaining the old hayrack in the hayloft above. The old horse trough remains but only plants drink from it nowadays. The 'snug' really is snug and seats 12. Business or private parties can be catered for. Summer sees the barbecue glowing in the garden, where there's a play area with shop and aviary, and children are welcome. Large car park.

THE RETREAT

Bocking Church Street, Braintree.   Tel. (0376) 47947

Location:	Just off A131 Halstead Road, opposite 11th century church.
Credit cards:	Access, Visa, Amex, Diners.
Accommodation:	Three twin rooms all en suite.
Bitters:	Adnams, Ruddles, Websters, Draught Guinness.
Lagers:	Carlsberg, Holsten, Fosters.

Examples of bar meals (lunch & evening, 7 days): *scallops with cream & cheese sauce, Yorkshire pudding filled with ham onion cheese & cream sauce, courgettes filled with onion tomato & garlic topped with melted cheese.*

Examples of restaurant meals (lunchtime every day except Saturday, & evenings except Sunday. Open for Sunday lunch until 4pm): *saute medallions of venison, steaks, vegetarian dishes, lobster thermidor, duck breast with Grand Marnier sauce, chicken breast with garlic ginger & yoghurt sauce.*

The aptly named Retreat is a picturesque 15th-century inn not far, but far enough, from the bustle that is Braintree. David & Margaret Locke have made changes in recent years: the restaurant is now a bar area with consequent increase in space. A conservatory joins two converted rooms making a restaurant seating up to 50, ideal for functions, business and those just seeking a meal that is imaginative and of high quality - Egon Ronay recommended. The large sheltered garden is nicely landscaped and enclosed for those with children of an adventurous nature, who will want to peer down the ancient 30ft well in one of the bars. There is a no-smoking area and a car park.

THE GREEN MAN

Gosfield, nr Halstead.   Tel. (0787) 472746
    Location: On Braintree to Hedingham road.
Credit Cards: Access, Visa.
     Bitters: Greene King.
     Lagers: Kronenbourg.

Examples of bar meals (lunchtime 7 days, every evening except Sunday):
Evenings: *game soup with sherry, breaded mushrooms with garlic butter, Dover sole, oxtail ragout, steaks, boiled beef & carrots, roast duck with orange sauce, plaice fillets with prawn sauce, steak & kidney pudding, vegetarian (e.g.spinach pancakes, vegetable lasagne)*. Lunchtime: *Cold buffet, hot dish of the day*.

Not East Anglia's most attractive pub from the outside but, as with people, appearance can be misleading. Venture inside and you will find yourself in a 16th-century oak beamed bar or dining area of considerable character. However, your eyes will be drawn immediately to the splendid buffet table, which looks ready to collapse under the weight of massive king prawns, fresh salmon, succulent roasts and more. This is supplemented at lunchtime by a hot dish of the day, and all is home cooked. Special requests are catered for, if possible, and bookings accepted. There's also a small function room for private parties. Children are tolerated if well behaved; if not, there's a rather nice garden by the large car park. Proprietor John Arnold can be proud of his successful well-run business, but modestly claims that colleague Janet Harrington, who supervises daily affairs, is the driving force behind it.

THE BELL INN

St. James Street, Castle Hedingham.   Tel. (0787) 60350
> Location: Village centre.
> Credit cards: Not accepted.
> Bitters: Greene King Abbot & IPA (gravity fed from barrel).
> Lagers: Heineken, Kronenbourg.

Examples of bar meals (lunch & evening, except Monday evenings): *steak &*
Guinness pie, shepherds pie, lasagne, smoked prawns with garlic dip, haddock & prawn
gratinee, grilled trout, sirloin steaks, lamb cutlets, Thai chicken curry, burgers,
ploughmans. Homemade treacle tart with toffee ice cream.

The beautiful village of Castle Hedingham is a suitable setting for this notable 15th
century inn. Previously having served as a magistrates court and a theatre, The Bell
is second only to the castle itself in what was historically an important village. Solid
oak beams, authentic brickwork and exposed wooden floorboards together create a
medieval air, whilst the fresh flowers, real ale from the barrel and friendly service
are all part of the charm for which the delightful old inn is renowned. Children are
welcome in two of the spacious bars and of course in the lovely walled orchard
garden (with croquet). Above the saloon bar is a great hall with a superbly restored
barrel ceiling, available for private hire. Live jazz (entry free) is held here on the last
Sunday lunchtime of each month. Large car park to the rear.

THE ROSE & CROWN

Nayland Road, Gt Horkesley, nr Colchester.

Tel. (0206) 271251
Fax (0206) 272977

Location: On A134 Colchester to Sudbury road.
Credit cards: Access, Visa.
Bitters: Greene King.
Lagers: Harp, Kronenbourg.

Examples of bar meals (lunch & evening, 7 days): *moules mariniere, Suffolk hotpot, game, steaks, fresh fish & seafood, ploughman's, sandwiches.*
Examples of restaurant meals (every evening, plus trad. Sun. roast): *spicy Cajun prawns, crispy coated vegetables with dip, beefsteak kidney & mushroom pie with Guinness, seafood pie, Indian style chicken, kleftico, pork & mustard sausages, steaks, poached salmon with tarragon sauce, trout stuffed with prawns & mushrooms, brown rice & hazelnut roast with redcurrant sauce, salads.*

A common name for a pub that is anything but: a huge and diverse menu, as appetising as it is imaginative, places this Rose and Crown amongst the aristocracy. As the photo shows, it also happens to be quite a handsome building, dating from around 1700, and is replete with exposed timbers and brickwork, open woodburner, rustic style furniture and various equine artefacts. The intimate 46-seater restaurant, formerly the wine cellar, is the scene of theme evenings, held throughout the year, a chance for chef Martin Duggan, who, with wife Penny, now manages the pub, to show the range of his talents. Children welcome. Barbecues are lit in the garden in season. Large car park.

THE COMPASSES INN

Ipswich Road, Holbrook.   Tel. (0473) 328332
    Location: On main road in village centre.
  Credit cards: Access, Visa, Diners, Amex.
     Bitters: Tolly Cobbold Original & Best, Tetley, Flowers Original.
     Lagers: Castlemaine, Stella Artois, Carlsberg.

Examples of bar meals (lunch & evening, 7 days): *chicken Kiev, chicken & mushroom tart, steak & mushroom pie, seafood lasagne, steaks, aubergine bake, spinach & mushroom lasagne, daily specials.*
Examples of restaurant meals (7 days): *stuffed mussels, poached salmon with butter sauce, rack of lamb, turkey cordon bleu, sirloin steak, prawn curry. Trad Sun lunch £9.75.*

Travellers once hired ponies here for the journey to Ipswich, which was a safer mode of transport than by boat on the River Orwell, to judge from the engraved ships' timbers dredged up and put on display. Also on display, hanging from the beams, are more than 1000 key fobs. The Victorian restaurant has an airy light atmosphere, a product of the high vaulted ceilings and great tall windows. However, what really makes the Compasses so popular are the generous portions at very reasonable prices. Continental visitors will feel welcome: EEC flags flutter outside and the menu is highlighted by the colours appropriate to each dish. The newly refurbished bar is on a split level with an eating area where children are allowed - they also have a play area overlooked by the restaurant. The more mature can relax in the garden or on the patio with a pint and a good meal. Features in national good pub guides.

THE SHIPWRECK BAR & RESTAURANT

Shotley Point Marina, Shotley Gate.   Tel. (0473) 788865

Location: At mouth of Rivers Orwell & Stour, 12 mins SE of Ipswich & A45.

Credit cards: Access, Visa, Eurocheques.

Bitters: Adnams, Sam Smiths, 2 weekly guests (from handpump).

Lagers: Carlsberg, Carlsberg Export. Plus Beamish, Strongbow.

Examples of bar/restaurant meals (lunch & evening 7 days, plus breakfasts 8-10:30am in season only): *homemade carrot & lentil soup, garlic king prawns, chilli, chicken korma, steaks, lasagne, steak & kidney pie, lamb hotpot, tuna steak with lemon & prawn cream sauce, smoked salmon a la King, scampi, cod, plaice, vegetable tagliatelle, jacket potatoes. Spotted dick, apple crumble, chocolate nut sundae. Children's menu.*

The view over Harwich and Felixstowe docks is magnificent, here at the confluence of two rivers. It certainly helps to draw custom from miles around, but since opening in April 1992, landlord George Field and staff have established The Shipwreck on its own merits, known for homecooked food served in ample portions and representing very good value. Built about 30 years ago, this former engineering workshop has been totally transformed. It's not hard to guess the theme; masts, sails, nets and an enormous mural depicting an underwater scene - nothing else would be appropriate in such a setting. Every Thursday throughout the year solo musicians perform, and there are other various functions and balls with live entertainment, held in function rooms of differing sizes. There's also a private bar, large family room and a vast, safe garden with barbecue.

BUTT AND OYSTER

Pin Mill, Chelmondiston, nr Ipswich.   Tel. (0473) 780764

Location:	Off B1456 Shotley Road.
Credit Cards:	Not accepted.
Bitters:	Tolly Cobbold - on handpump or from barrel, from the reborn brewery across the river. Occasional guests.
Lagers:	Castlemaine, Stella Artois.
Extended Hours:	Winter: Mon-Sat 11am-3pm, 7pm-11pm. Sun 12 noon-3pm, 7pm-10:30pm. Summer: Mon-Sat 11am-11pm. Sunday as winter.

Examples of bar meals (lunch & evening, 7 days): *fishermans pie, smoked chicken with onion & chive dip, savoury sausage pie, pork duck orange & walnut pie, steak & kidney pie, giant prawns, seafood platter, crispy curry pancakes, veal cordon bleu, farm manager's lunch, ravioli. Limited menus (rolls etc) outside main hours.*

Views of the River Orwell as this pub has are a major asset. However, not content to rest on nature's laurels, Dick and Brenda Mainwaring really work at keeping the Butt and Oyster authentic. The concept works, as national guides and newspapers testify. The locals also treasure it, and the elders will confirm that it is unchanged over 60 years. Even the pub games, some almost forgotten elsewhere, live on here; juke boxes and the like do not. The view from the bar and dining room overlooks the boats and river, and at very high tides the river nearly overlooks them. There's an old smoke room with bare floorboards and smoke-stained ceiling. The homecooked food varies daily and is of generous proportions. There's a children's room, or sit at tables by the river's edge.

THE ANGEL INN

Stoke by Nayland, nr Colchester. Tel. (0206) 263245

Location:	Village centre.
Credit cards:	Access, Amex, Diners, Visa.
Accommodation:	6 doubles, all en suite.
Bitters:	Adnams, Greene King.
Lagers:	Carlsberg, Kronenbourg.

Examples of bar meals (lunch & evening, 7 days): *griddled fresh fillet of grouper fish, baby artichokes in vinaigrette, fresh lobster, smoked fillets of trout, vegetable bake, medley of salads, saute of chicken livers with wine mushrooms & herbs. Large choice of blackboard specials changed twice daily.*

Examples of restaurant meals (evenings except Sunday & Monday): *homemade terrine of venison, poached comice pear with fresh scallops, quenelles of chicken with wild mushrooms, brochette of seafood, supreme of guinea fowl, vegetarian dish, speciality fresh griddled fish.*

Although the Georgian facade is pretty enough, it is but a prelude to the very splendid 17th century interior. Looking for the most outstanding feature, one would settle on the gallery which leads from the tastefully refurbished bedrooms to a view over the restaurant. A charming little lounge divides the bars from the two dining rooms, one of which has an ancient 40' well. The restaurant and pub are regularly feted by national guides (including Egon Ronay) for the sheer excellence of the food, which has made The Angel widely admired in the region. The village is a very pretty one, and just 15 minutes drive from Colchester.

THE BELL INN

The Street, Kersey. Tel/fax. (0473) 823229
Location: Village centre.
Credit cards: Access, Visa, Diners, Amex, Luncheon Vouchers.
Accommodation: 6 en suite doubles planned for late 1993. Restricted Caravan Club reg. site.
Bitters: From a selection of 35 rotating ales, plus draught Murphy's.
Lagers: Kronenbourg 1664, Castlemaine XXXX.

Kersey

Examples of bar meals (lunch & evening, 7 days): *feta cheese kebabs, seafood pineapple, daily fish, turkey & mushroom pie, steak & kidney pie, 24ozs rump steak, bangers & mash with thick onion gravy, chicken Kiev, Scotch salmon, mushroom & hazelnut pie, vegetable stroganoff. H/m apple & blackberry crumble, pancakes, profiteroles.*

Examples of restaurant meals (lunch & evening every day except Sunday. Trad. roast on Sun. 11:30am - 2pm): *savoury stuffed profiteroles, pineapple longboat, pork Cleopatra, lamb Catherine, duck Tropicale, lobster, lemon sole, steak Bordelaise, 5 vegetarian choices. Afternoon/CREAM teas April - Sept daily. Other months Sats & Suns only.*

"The prettiest village in the world" - a bold claim, but one to which many would subscribe. Once a coaching inn and still a handsome building inside and out, The Bell has shared the last 700 years with Kersey, and is said to be haunted. Visitors from the four corners beat a path, including film producers (Lovejoy, Campion, Witchfinder General) and hungry camera crews! Licensees Alex and Lynne Coote came here in summer '89, and their home cooking and bonhomie have kept a place in national good pub guides. Families welcome, and sunny patio and garden to rear. Parties well catered for.

SPECIAL OFFER: *Present this book on arrival for 15% off a 2-course meal and coffee Mon & Tues, 10% off Wed-Fri. Valid in both bar and restaurant, but not on Bank Hols.*

47

THE GEORGE & DRAGON

Hall Street, Long Melford.   Tel. (0787) 371285

Location:	Centre of village, on main road.
Credit cards:	Access, Visa, Mastercard.
Accommodation:	2 singles, 1 double, 1 twin, 1 family. £17.50pp. Single rooms £20pp. Weekend Breaks.
Bitters:	Greene King, Rayments.
Lagers:	Kronenbourg.

Examples of bar meals (lunch & evening, 7 days): *beef & Guinness pie, rabbit pie, curry, steak, chicken tagliatelle, crab salad, ploughman's (noted), sandwiches. Chocolate & rum bumble, plum crumble, sherry trifle.*

Examples of restaurant meals (as above): *liver cassis, herb pancake; venison steak with rich plum & cherry sauce, ribeye steak with bordelaise sauce, poached brill, whole plaice, mushroom stroganoff. Trad. Sun. roasts (booking advised).*

NB Open all day except Sundays.

"Not a pub, not a restaurant, but a true village inn" - the words of Peter, Marilyn and Ian Thorogood, who've revived the art of innkeeping at their 16th century coaching inn over the past seven years. That means "no karaoke, discos, keg beer or men in oversized suits drinking from bottles!" Instead, you have a warm, personal welcome, delicious and filling meals created in the kitchen from fine local produce, traditional local beers and superb French wines (clarets especially good). Entertainment, too, is traditional: bar billiards, darts, shut-the-box etc, plus occasional folk and jazz. Well-behaved children are welcome, and there is a garden. An ideal base to stay, right in the heart of the region, Long Melford is England's longest village, and one of the most famous. Recommended by most major pub guides.

THE HARE INN

High Street, Long Melford.   Tel. (0787) 310379
      Location: On the main road north of village, opp. Kentwell Hall,
                   signposted from new bypass.
   Credit cards: Access, Visa.
       Bitters: Greene King Abbot & IPA.
       Lagers: Kronenbourg, Harp.

Examples of bar meals (lunch & evening, 7 days): *Scotch salmon & cheese bake, mushroom & asparagus au gratin, steaks, mixed grill, grilled fish of day, scampi Newburgh, chicken princess (supreme with prawns & asparagus, finished with white wine & cream sauce), pork fillet Clementine (fillet with cointreau sauce, finished with fresh orange & cream), lasagne, veg. curry, taco flats, cottage pie, salads, sandwiches. Trad Sun roasts from £5.50 (booking advised).*

Long Melford is England's longest village, the parish church is a particularly fine (some say finest) example of its kind, and there are two stately homes (Melford Hall, Kentwell Hall) within yards of each other; all good reasons for a visit, but be sure to include The Hare in your itinerary. The facade is simple Georgian, but its Tudor origins are unmistakable inside. Imposing English oak beams span the ceiling and an open fire crackles invitingly, tables and chairs nestled snugly around it. John and Jill Pipe have presided for 12 years. They take special pride in their prime home produced Suffolk beef and local game in season, and east coast fish dishes are another speciality. Free seafood snacks are on the bar Sunday lunchtimes. Recommended by Egon Ronay. To the rear is a pleasant walled garden and parking. Family dining room.

THE PLOUGH INN

nr Kedington, nr Clare. Tel. (0440) 86789
Location: 1¹/₂ miles from Kedington towards Hundon. If in doubt, phone.
Credit cards: Access, Visa.
Accommodation: 6 rooms, all en suite. Caravan Club certified location.
Bitters: Nethergate, Bass IPA, Greene KIng.
Lagers: Carling, Tennents, Carlsberg, Warsteiner LA.

Examples of bar meals (lunch & evening from 6pm, 7 days): *trout & watercress pate, homemade soups, steak & kidney pie, fresh fish, steaks, ploughmans.*
Examples of restaurant meals (as above): *lemon sole with prawns, duckling breast with orange, steaks, salmon poached in wine & cream, vegetarian dishes, seafood night every Tuesday. Trad. Sun. roasts (booking advised).*

Some of the finest views in Suffolk are commanded from this elevated position, high over rolling countryside. For over 30 years The Plough has been in the hands of the Rowlinson family. Now celebrating their 10th anniversary here, David and Marion have carried out extensive but careful alterations to create a traditional country pub atmosphere, using soft red bricks and oak beams from an old barn. They added a new extension of six en suite bedrooms, have recently enlarged the lounge and installed a new food display counter. Whilst providing modern amenities (the restaurant is air conditioned, for example) it has been without sacrifice of old fashioned friendliness and charm. This and good home cooked food (seafood a speciality) has won a place in local affections and a number of major guides. Not an easy one to find, but patience reaps its rewards. Children welcome.

THE CHERRY TREE

Bury Road, Stradishall.   Tel. (0440) 820215

Location: On A143 Bury to Haverhill road.
Credit cards: Mastercard (only for bills over £10).
Accommodation: Facilities for caravans & campers, by arrangement.
Bitters: Greene King Abbott & IPA.
Lagers: Harp, Kronenbourg.

Examples from lunch menu (every day): *chicken sate with spicy peanut sauce, beef curry, toad in the hole, steaks, lasagne, macaroni cheese, French sticks, jacket potatoes, ploughman's, sandwiches. Trad Sun roasts £4.75 main course (booking advised).*
Examples from evening menu (every day): *beef Guinness & mushroom pie, gratin of smoked haddock with prawns, minted lamb in red wine, poached wild salmon, trio of lamb cutlets, mixed grill, steaks, vegetarian.*

One of the joys of exploring our lovely countryside is the occasional chancing upon a quite delightful little country pub. Here in the heart of rural Suffolk is one such. Set in three very pleasant acres, including a large fish pond (complete with resident ducks), this 16th century farmhouse became a pub only in 1943, taking the place of another which unfortunately was in the way of pilots taking off from RAF Stradishall! Since then there have been only four landlords, the latest being local people, Jane and Roger Marjoram, with 20 years experience in the trade. Their menus are a commendable blend of staple English favourites with a little foreign zest. Separate dining room. Children welcome in garden.

THE AFFLECK ARMS

Dalham, nr Newmarket Tel. (0638) 500306
Location: Village centre, 4¹/₂ miles south-east of Newmarket.
Credit Cards: Not accepted.
Bitters: Greene King.
Lagers: Harp, Kronenbourg.

Examples of bar meals (lunch & evening, 7 days): *homemade soups, steaks, chicken Kiev, homemade steak & kidney pie, grilled cod or plaice, seafood platter, omelettes, salads, daily specials. Sorbettes, raspberry special. Trad. Sun. roasts.*

80% of the houses in Dalham have a thatched roof - the highest rate anywhere in the country. If in Devon, say, it would be a tourist trap, but the genius of East Anglia is that it knows how to keep quiet about its many little treasures. Such a delightful village would not be complete without its old country pub, and this Elizabethan inn fulfills the role admirably. It's lovely to look at and seems to engender a remarkable atmosphere. Flowers on each table are a nice touch, and one can eat in any of three dining rooms. Children are welcome, and would enjoy the front garden, which has a pleasant river frontage, and the new Pets Corner to the rear of the car park. Barbara Markham has been running her "simple village pub" since May '88, and maintained its place in major guides.

THE PLOUGH

The Green, Rede, nr Bury St. Edmunds.   Tel. (028 489) 208
  Location: Cul de sac, not far from church.
Credit cards: Access, Visa.
    Bitters: Greene King.
     Lagers: Harp, Kronenbourg.

Examples of bar meals (lunchtime every day, & evenings except Sunday): *fresh fish (speciality), steaks, curries, salads, daily specials eg jugged hare in port & wine sauce, romany lamb with spaghetti & parmesan cheese, beef in horseradish sauce, chicken ham & stilton crumble.*
Examples of restaurant meals (evenings only, not Sundays. Traditional Sunday lunch): *pigeon breasts in Madeira & spinach, venison, trout, roast duck, veal in Dijon mustard & brandy, poached salmon, local game (speciality).*

Standing on the highest point in Suffolk, the Plough is looked up to in more senses than one. Its chocolate box prettiness never lapses into tweeness; the atmosphere is relaxed and unstuffy, and the home cooked food is good value and served in generous portions. Built around 1610, it occupies an exceptionally peaceful and lovely spot in a cul de sac by the village pond. One can sit here or at the back in the large sunny garden with a tropical aviary, a dovecote and ponies - children love it! They are welcome inside in the eating areas, but will probably not appreciate the superb inglenook, timber beams and fine collection of teapots. The separate restaurant has a good name, and the Plough is a regular in national guides. Your amiable hosts are Brian and Joyce Desborough.

THE WHITE HORSE

Rede Road, Whepstead, nr Bury St. Edmunds.   Tel. (0284) 735542
     Location: Outskirts of village, off A143.
  Credit cards: Not accepted.
      Bitters: Rayments, Greene King.
      Lagers: Harp, Stella Artois.

Examples of bar meals (lunch & evening, 7 days - revised daily): *steaks, Italian meatballs, Maylasian chicken, sweet'n'sour pork, mussels in cider, lamb paprika, beef & veg. curry, kebabs, fresh fish Friday & Saturday, salads, vegetarian dishes.*

Mauritian cooking dosen't often appear on the average bill of fare, but David and Rosemary Woolf do not run an average pub. Rosemary comes from Mauritius, and her authentic native style, utilising fresh produce, made her a finalist in the 1988 'Pub Caterer of the Year' award. The everchanging menu has an excitingly cosmopolitian look, but the pub itself is firmly in keeping with the best English traditions. It began as a farmhouse in the early 17th century, becoming a public house in the early 1800s when the landlords brewed their own beer. The timber beams which supported the building then still do so now, and real fires glow in the inglenooks in winter. Slightly awkward to find, being a mile or so from the village centre, but well worth it. Children are welcome in the large garden, and inside if aged over five. Recommended by CAMRA guide.

THE MASON'S ARMS

14 Whiting Street, Bury St Edmunds.   Tel. (0284) 753955
      Location: Town centre.
   Credit cards: Not accepted.
       Bitters: Greene King.
       Lagers: Kronenbourg, Harp.

Examples of bar meals (lunch & evening, 7 days): *roast beef, lasagne, chilli, toad in the hole, scampi, plaice, cod, tagliatelle with garlic onions & cream, Yorkshire specials, cauliflower cheese, Chinese spring rolls, vegetable curry, salads, ploughman's, sandwiches, jacket potatoes, daily specials eg Japanese prawns, fresh lobster, crab, mussels.*

Stately Bury St Edmunds has many fine buildings gracing its elegant streets, but it cannot be generally said to be well endowed with good pubs. Happily, here is one exception, in a quiet side street, and easily picked out by the Essex weatherboarding, unusual in this area. The pub's rich history, dating from 1731, is described in a free leaflet available at the bar, and look for the selection of ancient herbal remedies. The collection of old beer taps is appropriate for a pub with a fine reputation for hand-pulled beers, also popular for good food, fresh seafood being a speciality. Chris and Jane Warton took over in '89, and welcome well behaved children. Barbecues are lit in the large patio/garden in summer (weather permitting). Parking could be tricky, but it's an easy walk from the town centre.

THE FOX

The Street, Pakenham, nr Bury St Edmunds.
      Tel. (0359) 30347

    Location: Village centre.
Credit cards: Access, Visa, Mastercard.
      Bitters: Greene King.
      Lagers: Harp, Kronenbourg.

Examples of bar meals (lunchtime & evening, 7 days): *chicken tagliatelle, canneloni, seafood tortelli, curries, Pakenham pie, steak & kidney in Abbot ale. Children's menu.* Examples of restaurant meals (every evening, plus trad. Sun. lunch): *steaks, mixed grill, gammon, many various vegetarian dishes.*

It may surprise you that this is seemingly the only village in Europe with both a watermill and windmill - one for 'trivia' fans. It is also distinguished by this well liked country pub, acquired only in December 1992 by Howard and Lynden Taylor. Lynden is a lecturer in home economics and catering, but both are very experienced, having previously run an hotel and restaurant in Scotland. Their standard is imaginative country cuisine at its best, utilising fresh, local seasonal produce, carefully prepared and presented. The partly beamed bar, split by an open brick fireplace, feels very '19th century', but more remarkable is the Reading Room restaurant, with a unique, peaceful atmosphere, attributable to the fact that it was indeed once a reading room. The pleasant garden is bordered by a stream with ducks. Live Country and Western is performed live in summer (barbecues by arrangement). Children welcome and dogs on leads.

THE CROWN HOTEL

104 High Street, Bildeston.   Tel. (0449) 740510
      Location: Village centre.
      Credit cards: Access, Visa.
      Accommodation: 15 rooms (1 with 4-poster), most en suite & with tv's. From
            £20 single, £30 double incl.
      Bitters: Adnams, Mauldon's Black Adder, Marston's Pedigree,
            Nethergate.
      Lagers: Carlsberg, Castlemaine, Warsteiner.

Examples of bar meals (lunch & evening, 7 days): *steak sandwich, eggs piperade, scampi, omelettes, ploughman's, sandwiches.*
Examples of restaurant meals (as above): *homemade taramasalata with warm mini baguette, butterbeans with spring onion & tuna tossed in light mayonnaise; chicken stroganoff, Victoriana Diable (sliced meats), oriental pork fillet, steaks, spinach fieullette in puff pastry with creamed spinach & leek sauce, fresh fish of day. Trad. Sun. roasts (booking advised).*

Once known as the 'most haunted public house in Britain', this eye-catching 15th century former merchant's house and coaching inn is far from spooky. Over the past few years it has been carefully restored to its former glory, and the splendid interior fully realises the promise of the striking timbered frontage: leaded lights, huge inglenooks, superbly furnished bedrooms, cosy bar and restaurant. Cuisine is of a standard to match, yet prices most affordable. The large, secluded garden has also benefitted from care and attention, and makes a very pleasant spot to sit and take the country air - for this is a lovely part of the county, well placed as a base from which to explore. Darts and crib in public bar. Well behaved children welcome. Large car park.

THE FOUR HORSESHOES

The Street, Whatfield, nr Ipswich   Tel. (0473) 827971
            Location: 2 miles off Hadleigh by-pass.
        Credit cards: Not accepted.
              Bitters: Greene King, Adnams, Nethergates, occasional guest.
              Lagers: Carlsberg, Carlsberg Export.

Examples of bar meals (lunchtimes Tues – Sat, evenings Fri & Sat, plus trad. Sun. roasts): *special steak & kidney pie in ale, chicken & mushroom pie, poacher's pie, lamb & apricot pie, shepherd's pie, steaks, chilli, lasagne, pasta dishes, pizzas, vegetarian dishes, baked filled potatoes, sandwiches, ploughman's, salads.*

Drive through the small farming village of Whatfield and you will discover the Four Horseshoes Inn, known locally as the 'Shoes'. You will find a cosy 17th Century timbered inn, comprising the tap room with its display of intriguing curiosities and collectables, large open fire, piano and comfortable lounge bar leading to the beer garden. Good home cooked food is served most of the time. Pool, crib, shove half penny and other traditional pastimes are still played. On Monday nights step back to Napoleonic times for a little harmless megalomania, as the local war gaming club meet to re-enact past battles. To assist in generating the right atmosphere the lounge bar is decorated with various military artefacts and prints. Other regular events are entertaining quiz evenings held on alternate Tuesdays. The Classic Motorcycle Club gather for their monthly meetings and Morris dancers shake a leg here once a year. Philip Hatch, landlord since 1988, welcomes well-behaved children, dogs and hikers. He is delighted to be recommended in The Good Beer Guide.
SPECIAL OFFER: FREE PUDDING WITH MAIN LUNCHTIME MEAL ON PRESENTATION OF THIS GUIDE.

THE BEAGLE

Old Hadleigh Road, Sproughton, Ipswich.   Tel. (0473) 730455

Location: Cul de sac next to new road, near Post House Hotel.
Credit cards: Access, Visa, Amex.
Bitters: Adnams, Greene King, Theakstons, Mauldons, guests.
Lagers: Becks, Kronenbourg, Carlsberg, Kaliber.

Examples of bar meals (lunchtime only every day except Sunday): *homemade soup, pate, parma ham with melon, local smoked kippers, liver & sausage casserole, cheese & vegetable pie, steak & kidney pie, chilli, ploughmans, farmers lunch, prawns, duck breast, sirloin, chicken & ham pie. Coffee & brandy gateau, cherry crumble.*

Painstakingly converted from four cottages just a few years ago, The Beagle is now a firm local favourite, and quickly won a placed in Egon Ronay's guide. To become so well established so quickly indicates a lot of imagination and hard work. The interior confirms this: two superb inglenooks take pride of place among the exposed beams and the whole is most pleasing, as the usually quite full car park will testify (fortunately, there's ample parking). There is no children's room as such, but there is an extension in the shape of a conservatory onto the lounge where children over five are permitted. The garden is of course still there for sunnier days. William and Nicola Freeth extend a warm welcome and cordially invite you to try their delicious homecooked fare.

THE MAYBUSH INN

Waldringfield, nr Woodbridge. Tel. (047 366) 215
Location: Riverside, at end of village.
Credit Cards: Not accepted.
Bitters: Tolly Cobbold.
Lagers: Labatt's, Hansa Export, Hansa, Tennents LA.

Examples of lunchtime meals (7 days, not Christmas or Boxing day): *home cooked meats, 'ploughpersons' lunch, peeled cold water prawns, pork & egg pie, cod & haddock fillets, dish of the day.*
Examples of evening meals (as above): *some dishes as lunchtime, plus breaded chicken breast stuffed with cream cheese & mushrooms, chicken Kiev, golden seafood assortment, shell-on prawns.*

No doubt about it, The Maybush enjoys one of the most spectacular locations of any pub in the region, on the shores of the wide river Deben. The 150 seater garden reaches down to the water's edge, and affords breathtaking views in both directions - reason enough for a visit but, almost as a bonus, the pub itself is first rate. The large bar overlooks the river, so you can feast your eyes whilst treating your taste buds to traditional, wholesome food in a cheering, hospitable environment. A popular family pub, the car park is often well filled, and customers travel from afar; there's no passing traffic, for The Maybush is at the end of a long narrow country lane, very pleasant for a stroll.

THE RAMSHOLT ARMS

Dock Road, Ramsholt, nr Woodbridge.   Tel. (0394) 411229
  Location: Off B1083 Woodbridge-Bawdsey road.
  Credit cards: Not accepted.
  Bitters: Adnams, guests.
  Lagers: Carlsberg, Carlsberg Export. Good selection of bottled beers
  & lagers. Also excellent selection of traditional & New World
  wines.

Examples of bar meals (lunch & evening, 7 days. Extended hours in summer):
Lunch (summer): cold meats, homemade pies, fish & salad bar, fresh lobster, Dover sole (speciality when available), catch of the day, steaks & h/m burgers (speciality). Winter: hot daily specials, extensive menu including steaks, Sunday roasts.
Evenings: *large choice of starters, main courses & desserts. Vegetarian & vegan dishes: wide variety served lunch & evening.*

No photograph can really do justice to one of East Anglia's finest riverside freehouses, on a wide sweep of the river Deben with unsurpassed views in both directions. Standing at the end of a long country lane, the pub has two car parks, a lovely sandy beach for the children (swimming at high tide) and a beautiful terrace with seating for 200. Inside you'll find two bars and a dining room (known as the Colonel's Room). Built around 1747 as a ferryman's cottage and Dock farm, it was used as a shooting lodge in the 50's and 60's - royalty has stayed here. Recommended by nearly all the national guides and several national newspapers. If coming by water contact harbour master George Collins, to be found on the quay.

61

THE KING'S HEAD

Orford, nr Woodbridge.   Tel. (0394) 450271

Location:	Village centre, next to church.
Credit cards:	Diners.
Accommodation:	4 doubles, 1 twin, 1 family, with tv & tea & coff. £19.50 pp per night. Special winter breaks.
Bitters:	Adnams Bitter, Broadside, Old, Tally Ho, Extra & Mild.
Lagers:	Carling, Skol, Carlsberg Export.

Examples of bar meals (lunch & evening, 7 days): *monkfish & lobster souffle, fresh local lobster, scallops in sherry & mushroom sauce, homemade fish pie, cod, king-sized prawns in garlic sauce, sirloin steak, crabs, mussels, lemon sole etc in season.*

Examples of restaurant meals (evenings except Sun. & Thurs.): *many dishes as above, turbot in scallop & garlic sauce, wild duck in red wine & cranberry sauce, lobster thermidor, local specialities when available eg bass, brill, mullet, salmon trout, Dover sole, skate, samphire.*

NB Open all day Bank Hols and Saturdays in high season.

Orford is famed for its oysters, and seafood predominates at this celebrated 13th century smugglers inn, personally run by the Shaw family (currently Alistair and Joy) for over 25 years. Alistair derives great pleasure from his individual and creative preparations, as do his customers, including some well known faces, who return again and again, and all the major guides have little but praise. It seems an old lady keeps coming back, too, in spectral form! Children are welcome in dining room or small garden. If you have the foresight to book a room, you could enjoy a superb breakfast in bed (optional) of grilled lemon sole or ham, then a stroll around this delightful village.

YE OLD CROSS KEYS

Crabbe Street, Aldeburgh.   Tel. (0728) 452637
      Location: Seafront, by lifeboat.
  Credit cards: Not accepted.
       Bitters: Adnams.
       Lagers: Lowenbrau, Carling, Castlemaine. James White cider.

Examples of bar meals (lunch & evening, 7 days): *homemade steak & kidney pie, lamb hotpot, seafood pancakes, oysters, lobster, crab, salmon, ploughman's. Jam roly-poly (noted).*

Aldeburgh is one of the prettiest seaside towns on the east coast, and is of course famed for its music festival in June. Another very good reason to visit is this super little 16th century pub, tucked away between the main street and sea front. It looks every inch the fisherman's haunt it once was, and the nautical flavour extends to the home cooked meals, local seafood being the speciality. Graham and Jenny upgraded levels of comfort a few years ago when they took over, without loss of essence. The solid inglenook, dividing the bar into two, remains the centre piece. To the rear is a bright, clean food bar which leads out to a small, sheltered garden (children permitted) with plenty of tables and chairs and views out to sea. A devout local following makes it advisable to arrive early in summer. Rated by Les Routiers and other national guides. Large car park nearby.

THE LION INN

Main Road, Little Glemham, nr Woodbridge. Tel. (0728) 746505
>   Location: On A12 between Woodbridge and Saxmundham.
>   Credit cards: Access, Visa, Mastercard, Switch.
>   Bitters: Adnams, House ale, Websters, guests.
>   Lagers: Carlsberg, Castlemaine.

Examples of bar/restaurant meals (lunch & evening, 7 days): *homemade soup, steaks & grills, all-day breakfast, luxury whole-tail scampi, homemade pies, curry, chilli, homecooked ham, trout, veg lasagne, egg curry, mushroom & nut fettucini, filled jacket potatoes, salads, ploughman's, baps. Homemade chunky apple pie, spotted dick, treacle & chocolate sponge puddings, cherry pavlova. Tea, coffee, drinking chocolate. Children's menu. 3-course trad. Sun. roasts from £5.50 (booking advised).*

The lonely blasted beaches, eerily silent estuaries and oozing marshlands of this 'Heritage Coast' are balm to a troubled soul, but the body still requires sustenance, and that is the forte of Peter and Pauline Fry. Pauline and her two colleagues have done all the cooking over the past five years, furthering a tradition of hospitality on this site which stretches back to Domesday. The grade II listed building is graced by exposed timbers (some taken from a 16th-century boat), brick fireplace, wrought iron ballustrading, cottagey furnishings and paintings by a local artist (for sale). Pool, skittles, darts and other traditional games are played, and extra fun is to be had on Harvest Supper, Halloween and other nights, plus occasional barbecues in summer. Well-behaved children are welcome, and the garden has an aviary and rabbits. Small private parties catered for.

THE CRETINGHAM BELL

Cretingham, nr Otley, nr Woodbridge.   Tel. (0728) 685419
       Location: 4 miles from Otley, 12 miles from Woodbridge.
   Credit cards: Visa, Mastercard.
        Bitters: Adnams, Charles Wells, guests.
        Lagers: Lowenbrau, Castlemaine, Carlsberg.

Examples of bar meals (lunch & evening, 7 days): *deep fried potato skins filled with cheese & crispy bacon, barbecue ribs, giant Yorkshire pudding filled with Suffolk sausages & onion gravy, pork in apple sauce with vegetables topped with suet pastry, chicken & mushroom pie, steak & kidney pie, curry, chilli, char-grills, finnan haddie pie, catch of the day, trio bean bake, crank's nut roast, farmer's lunch, blackboard specials. Children's menu.*

The mouthwatering menu reflects the best kind of English cooking, but there are many other attractions at this very popular 16th century pub. Families are well looked after: there's a family room, the garden has a playframe and new licensees Jackie and Terry Bywater are pleased to cater for birthday parties, anniversaries etc - try one of chef's delicious liquor sponge cakes. Coach parties are also welcome by arrangement. A private room may be hired for business meetings at any time, and outside catering (with bar) is a speciality - worth bearing in mind for a wedding (marquees available). Live jazz is performed on the first Tuesday of each month, and barbecues are held on Sundays throughout the summer. Recommended by national good pub guides.
SPECIAL OFFER: 10% OFF BOTTLE OF WINE FOR TWO PEOPLE DINING (NOT SATURDAY) ON PRODUCTION OF THIS GUIDE.

THE FALCON INN

Earl Soham, nr Framlingham.   Tel. (0728) 685263
        Location: Village centre (country setting), on A1120.
   Credit cards: Not accepted.
Accommodation: 4 rooms, BTB & Brittany Ferries approved. £18 pp incl.
         Bitters: Adnams, Greene King.
         Lagers: Kronenbourg, Harp.

Examples of bar meals (lunch & evening, 7 days. Limited menu Sunday lunchtime, due to popularity of 3 course lunch at £6.95 approx): *steak & kidney pie (featured in local paper), home cooked gammon, curries, ploughmans.*
Examples of restaurant meals (evenings only, Mon. - Sat.): *venison in red wine, rump steak (noted), beef bourgignon, chicken Kiev, vegetarian choices.*
NB *Morning coffee and homemade scones.*

England is noted for country pubs and good breakfasts, and you get both in good measure at this well preserved 15th century free house, replete with ancient timbers, log fire and other period features. Paul and Lavina Algar and staff proffer a warm welcome and a range of mostly homecooked meals. In summer the large garden is a sunny spot for lunch, and children are welcome any time in the pleasant restaurant, with crisp linen and flowers on every table. From the smart bedrooms you can gaze out over a bowling green and the open fields of Earl Soham, winner of the "Best Kept Village" award, and well placed to tour Framlingham Castle, Dunwich, Southwold and nearby animal and bird sanctuaries. If you are touring further afield, this being the heart East Anglia, Sandringham is only 1¹/₂ hours, and Constable Country just one hour. Functions catered for. Coaches by apptmnt.

THE BUCK'S HEAD

Thwaite, nr Eye.   Tel. (0449) 766219
        Location: On A140 towards to Diss.
    Credit cards: Visa, Diners, Amex.
        Bitters: Greene King, Boddingtons, Flowers Best, guest.
        Lagers: Stella Artois, Heineken. Scrumpy Jack cider.

Examples from bar/restaurant menu (lunch & evening Mon - Sat, plus Sun. roast): *steaks & grills, curries, beef Wellington, duck a l'orange, venison in red wine, veal cordon bleu, lemon sole, cod, plaice, scampi, king ribs, vegetable lasagne/chilli, salads, ploughman's, sandwiches, chicken specials eg chicken Napoleon (in brandy sauce), chicken calabrai (cauliflower cheese), daily specials eg steak & kidney pie, sausage & bacon casserole. Mississippi mud pie, treacle & walnut flan, cherry cheesecake. Children's menu. Trad. Sun. roasts £4.25 (booking advised).*

New licensees Roger and Sharon took up the reigns here only in April 1992, and extend a warm welcome to their cottagey 15th century pub. They have not been slow to make their mark and in particular are making the pub more family-oriented. Children have their own menu, a full playground (including bouncing castle) in the garden, and there will be regular barbecues during the summer. Prices are kept most affordable. Of particular interest inside in the single beamed bar is the walk-through fireplace, covered in horse brasses. An inglenook takes pride of place in the cosy little restaurant. Indoor amusements consist of a pool table and dominoes. Ample parking.

THE TROWEL & HAMMER

Mill Road, Cotton, nr Stowmarket.   Tel. (0449) 781234
      Location: Village outskirts (near Bacton).
   Credit cards: Not accepted.
       Bitters: Adnams, Greene King, Whitbread.
       Lagers: Stella Artois, Heineken.

Examples of bar meals (lunch & evening, 7 days): *kleftiko, moussaka, steaks, kebabs, scampi, salads, sandwiches, ploughman's.*
Examples of restaurant meals (as above): *succulent scotch & local steaks cooked to your satisfaction, mixed grill, tornedos Rossini, steak Diane, East Anglian trout, Dover sole, king prawn in garlic butter, half duck in cherry brandy sauce. Trad. Sun. lunch £11 (3 courses + coffee. Appetising salads of fresh local vegetables. Last food orders 10:30pm weekdays, 10pm Sundays.*

On the front cover of one of our previous editions, this 'Pub of the Year' (as elected two years running by readers of a well known local newspaper) could never be described as commonplace. Even in this area, so well endowed with beautiful buildings, it is exceptionally handsome and enticing. Few others can boast an outdoor pool in large colourful gardens, an invaluable asset in long hot summers. The water doesn't look quite so inviting in January, of course, but there are plenty of other reasons for coming here.
Inside fully lives up to the promise of the exterior. At the end of the L-shaped bar is a superb floodlit inglenook, making its own special contribution to a warm, comfortable atmosphere. There's also the indoor pool - the kind you play on a flat table - in the games room. The 40-seater oak beamed restaurant, tastefully decorated, offers outstanding fresh food at very reasonable prices. One of the favourites, for which diners travel miles, is the mouthwatering 'kleftiko', a 1½lb piece of lamb cooked for six hours until falling off the bone, tender and succulent, and amazing value at £5.75 (at time of writing), including chips and salad.
Partners George and Chris are most amicable hosts, who have brought their Greek origins to bear fruitfully here in the heart of Suffolk. Naturally, everything on the menu is prepared in the kitchen, including houmous and taramosalata, but it would not be accurate to identify this as a Greek restaurant, as there are to be found many international and traditional English dishes also.
First-time visitors are invited to ring for directions before leaving home.

The Trowel & Hammer, Cotton.

THE WHITE HORSE INN

Station Road, Finningham, nr Stowmarket.   Tel. (0449) 781250

Location: Turn off A140 at Stoke Ash, or off A45 at Haughley.
Credit cards: Not accepted (at time of going to print).
Bitters: Tolly Original, Tetley, Flowers IPA.
Lagers: Labat, Castlemaine.

Examples of bar/restaurant meals (lunch & evening, 7 days): *homemade soup, garlic mushrooms on toast, steaks, all-day breakfast, h/m steak & kidney pudding, h/m lasagne, scampi, salads, ploughman's, sandwiches, h/m daily specials. Homemade cheesecake, chocolate fudgecake, Bakewell tart, jam roly poly, apple pie, icecream sundaes. Children's menu. Trad. Sun. roasts (booking advised).*

Character, that most elusive of assets, is a staple commodity here in this charming village, and particularly in its 15th century coaching inn. Old timbers, Victorian pictures, brasses, cottagey furniture and open fireplaces combine to pleasing effect. Locals say that previous landlords have all seen the ghost of a lady seated in the bar, but since their arrival in September 1991 (from The Four Horseshoes, Thornham Magna) Malcolm and Caroline Moore have breathed new life into the old place. Home cooking - from Caroline and sister Marie Ruth - is the main draw; time-honoured favourites like steak and kidney pudding and jam roly poly are many customers' first choice. One may enjoy it either in the 30-seater restaurant or the bar (including a cosy snug with barrels for seats); the menu and prices are the same. Special menus are laid on for theme evenings such as Halloween or Valentine. Children are welcome if eating or in the garden.

THE RAILWAY TAVERN

Mellis, nr Eye.   Tel. (0379) 783416
           Location: Signposted off A140 and A143 near Diss.
        Credit cards: Not accepted.
      Accommodation: 2 doubles. £25, or £15 as single incl. Weekend breaks £42.50
                       Stay 1 week and 1 day is free.
            Bitters: Adnams, Toby.
             Lagers: Carlsberg, Carlsberg Export & others.

Examples of bar meals (lunch & evening, 7 days): *homemade steak & kidney pie,
sausage liver & bacon hotpot, shepherds pie, lasagne, game pie, chicken/rabbit fricasee,
rabbit pie, sirloin steak, moussaka, ploughman's, sandwiches. Trad. Sun. roasts. Fresh
fruit & vegetables grown locally.*
NB All day opening (Sundays 12 - 3pm, 7 - 10:30pm) - some food always available.

From the unlikely background of a pig farm next to the main runway at Heathrow,
Enid (a former entomologist at the Natural History Museum, Kensington) and Fred
Peacock escaped to the tranquility of East Anglia in April 1992. Once the railway
hotel, their 18th century acquisition had been closed for a year. Encouraged by
locals dismayed at losing all three village pubs, they quickly restored the building
and the business, and attracted a favourable review from the Daily Telegraph in
September 1992 - quite an achievement in three months of trading. They have a
pool team and sponsor the local football and cricket teams, but it is principally for
the homecooked fare for which they are winning acclaim. Children are welcome;
there's no garden, but Mellis has one of the largest village greens in Suffolk. Pool,
darts, shove ha'penny and other traditional games. Ideal riding, walking and cycling
country, just two miles from Thornham Walks.

THE FOUR HORSESHOES

Wickham Road, Thornham Magna, nr Eye.   Tel. (037 971) 777

Location:	400 yards off A140.
Credit cards:	Access, Visa, Diners, Amex.
Accommodation:	5 doubles, 1 twin, 2 singles, all en suite. Weekend Specials 3 nights for price of 2 - ring for details.
Bitters:	Adnams, Courage Directors, Websters, John Smiths, guests.
Lagers:	Holsten, Fosters, Carlsberg.

Examples of bar meals (lunch & evening, 7 days): *fisherman's hotpot, homemade pies (eg chicken ham & mushroom, apricot & walnut), country grill, vegetable & nut cutlets, salads, ploughman's, sandwiches, daily specials. Shoes' special banana split.*
Examples of restaurant meals (lunch & evening, 7 days): *grilled cod with stilton cheese, well hung steaks, guinea fowl forestiere, fresh lobster & other specialities to order, vegetarian choice. Many desserts. Trad. Sun. lunch (booking advised).*

One of the best known inns in East Anglia, 'The Shoes' is always lively and bustling. As the pictures suggest, it is the archetypal dream thatched cottage, a delight on the eye inside and out. The massive low beams and mud and daub walls suggest great age - over 800 years, in fact. It is the kind of place that has visitors from North America and Australasia wide eyed. The natives are less easily impressed by antiquity; they come more for the abundance of good food from a wide choice, both in bar and restaurant. The current management, which took over only in summer 1990, have had the good sense not to tamper too much with what was already a successful formula.

The bedrooms are luxurious, and residents have their own lounge. Dogs are permitted by arrangement (not in restaurant or bar), and well behaved children are welcome - cots are provided for the very young. This is a lovely area to explore: nearby Thornham Park is full of wild deer and rare orchids, ideal for a quiet stroll. Thornham Parva church is worth seeing for its uncommon medieval wall paintings and thatched roof. One is also well placed to travel further afield: north to Norwich and the Broads, east to the coast, south to Ipswich and Constable Country, and west to Bury St Edmunds, Newmarket and Cambridge.

THE DUKE OF MARLBOROUGH

Bury Road, Hepworth.   Tel. (0359) 51955
     Location: On A143, midway between Bury St Edmunds and Diss.
  Credit cards: Visa, Mastercard, Diners.
      Bitters: Greene King, Adnams, Mauldons.
      Lagers: Harp, Kronenbourg.

Examples of bar meals (lunch & evening, 7 days): *chicken satay & dip, crispy mushrooms & dip, steaks, mixed grill, tandoori chicken breast, steak & ale pie, chilli, lasagne, seafood lasagne, fisherman's platter, mushroom & nut fettucini, salads, sandwiches, ploughman's, daily specials, weekend evening specials. Daily set lunch approx. £4.50 (2 courses). Trad. Sun. roasts £4.95.*

New licensees took up the reins here in March 1992 - not the most auspicious time to enter the pub trade - but they have come armed with a qualification from The Institute of Innkeepers and plenty of enthusiasm. They have with their own hands refurbished the 250-year-old timbered building, warmed from two beautiful open fireplaces and furnished cottage-style. One old hand is Sid, a previous landlord who took the pub on at the age of 80 and lingers on in spirit, unaware his number has been called. Perhaps he enjoys the fortnightly quiz nights or the live music most Fridays or Saturdays. There's a family room for children and the garden has play equipment and barbecue - Pleasurewood Hills, Bressingham and the Broads are not too far. An adjacent field is for caravans. But most important, especially in current circumstances, is the very large helpings of good food at modest prices.

THE CROSS KEYS

The Street, Redgrave, nr Diss.   Tel. (0379) 898510
    Location: Village centre, on B1113 between South Lopham & Botesdale.
  Credit cards: Access, Visa.
     Bitters: Adnams, Greene King.
      Lagers: Castlemaine, Carlsberg, Harp, Kronenbourg.

Examples of bar meals (lunch & evening, 7 days): *chicken tikka, butterfly prawns, homemade steak/chicken pie, steaks, gammon with pineapple, mushroom & cashew nut pilaff, vegetable sausage, ploughman's, sandwiches, daily specials. Nut pie, treacle sponge, chocolate fudgecake, fruit pie. Children's menu. Trad. Sun. roasts (booking advised).*
NB Tues - Thurs one-course lunch £2.95 for senior citizens.

This freehouse is exemplary of the traditional, family-run country inn which, let's hope, will thrive for another 500 years at least. That's how long The Cross Keys has opened its doors to a hungry, thirsty public. For the last four the warm welcome has come from Eric (vice chairman of Licensed Victuallers) and Jackie Mackintosh, and it is extended to well-behaved children. Morris dancers entertain three or four times a year (including Christmas), but live folk music is a regular feature on the third Thursday of every month, and Sunday is quiz night. Other diversions include pool, darts, crib, dice and dominoes. Most prefer to sit and savour staple homecooked food (a la Jackie) in an agreeable atmosphere - two log fires, lots of beams and brasses. In summer the fire is lit under the barbecue in the garden. Blooms of Bressingham, Banham Zoo and Kilverstone Wildlife Park are all very close at hand.

THE SWAN

Hoxne, nr Eye.   Tel. (037 975) 275

     Location: Village centre.
Credit Cards: Not accepted.
      Bitters: Adnams, Greene King Abbott, Tetleys. Plus mild.
      Lagers: Carlsberg, Lowenbrau, Labatt.

Examples of bar meals (lunch & evening Mon - Fri, plus Sat lunch, plus trad Sun lunch in winter, cold buffet in summer): *homemade soups, haddock & prawn gratinee, pancake mushrooms & cheese, Lancashire hotpot, baked stuffed avocado, sandwiches.* Examples from dining room menu (Sat. evenings only): *herby brie parcels, roast partridge with braised red cabbage & chestnuts, scampi provencale, lamb cutlets in herby breadcrumbs, vegetarian by request. Rich chocolate pudding with fudge sauce, apple & calvados pancake.*

Time has marched slowly through the village of Hoxne (pronounced 'Hoxon'), and nowhere has it trod more softly than The Swan. Oak floors and beams, huge inglenooks - words bareley do justice to the superb 15th century interior, lovingly preserved by Frances and Tony Thornton-Jones. Once a coaching inn, careful refurbishment has provided a level of comfort which provides an exemplary blend of change without destruction. The honourable tradition regarding food is still observed; good and fresh and at very reasonable prices - from a bowl of soup to a three course meal. There's a games room with pool and shove ha'penny, and a croquet lawn in the garden. Well behaved children welcome. Recommended by national guides.

THE CRATFIELD POACHER

Bell Green, Cratfield, nr Halesworth.   Tel. (0986) 798206

        Location: 15 miles due west of Southwold.
 Credit cards: Not accepted.
       Bitters: Adnams, Greene King, guests.
       Lagers: Red Stripe, Carlsberg, Carlsberg Export, Fosters,
                  Stella Artois.

Examples of bar meals (lunch & evening, 7 days): *macaroni cheese, savoury pancake roll, chicken Kiev, sirloin steak, poacher pie, seafood platter, ploughman's, sandwiches, daily blackboard specials. Homemade desserts.*

As the picture suggests, this is no ordinary pub. The giant gorilla was the star of one of many special parties (including, on one occasion, a beach party, for which tons of sand were imported!) Landlord Graham Barker, who with wife Elaine has served here for 11 frantic years, is blessed with a genius for such bizarre, slightly lunatic but extremely popular stunts. His fertile imagination has been the force behind parachute jumps, scuba diving, windsurfing, raft racing, Christmas in July etc, raising many a laugh and pounds for charity in the process. But there is a more serious side: The Poacher is recommended by leading good beer and pub guides, and food is of a high standard. Some 1700 miniatures, all full, are joined by a collection of jubilee ales, some bottles being over 200 years old. Children are very welcome, and have an excellent play area in the garden.

THE WHITE HORSE

Badingham, nr Framlingham. Tel. (0728 75) 280
Location: On A1120 Stowmarket to Yoxford road.
Credit Cards: Not accepted.
Bitters: Adnams Best, Broadside, Tetleys, mild.
Lagers: Lowenbrau, Castlemaine.

Examples of bar meals (lunch & evening 7 days. Open all day July & Aug): *homemade pies, lasagne verdi, steaks, chilli, vegetarian dishes (speciality), blackboard specials eg carbonnade of beef, Emmett's award-winning ham, rhubarb crumble, death by chocolate. Afternoon teas. Children's menu.*
Examples of restaurant meals (lunch & evening, 7 days): *steaks, chicken Kiev, trout & almonds, venison in red wine, homemade vegetarian dishes. Homemade bread & butter pudding, Bakewell tart, sticky toffee pudding (speciality) & more. Trad. Sun. lunch.*

Alan and Eileen Doughty are Suffolk people, running a handsome 15th century Suffolk pub. They have introduced all day opening during July and August, so you can enjoy afternoon tea with homemade cakes or scones. Menus include vegetarian options, increasingly a house speciality, and the 30 seater restaurant is noted for its intimate atmosphere. The two bars, with a collection of rural artefacts and large inglenooks, are not lacking in character. Neither is the landlady, who is as warm in her welcome as she is strict about standards - only the best fresh vegetables, for example. Darts and pool are played inside, while the garden now has swings, climbing frames, a slide and scramble net. Next door the bowling green offers more sedate pleasures. Featured in leading national good pub guides.

THE CROWN AT WESTLETON

Westleton, Saxmundham.

Tel. (072 873) 777
Fax (072 873) 239

Location:	Village centre.
Credit cards:	Access, Amex, Diners, Visa.
Accommodation:	17 doubles, 2 singles, private facilities in all. AA 2* 72%. Tourist Board 4 stars commended.
Bitters:	Adnams, Greene King, Sam Smiths, Bombadier.
Lagers:	Carlsberg, Tuborg Gold. Plus Scrumpy Jack cider.

Examples of bar meals (lunchtime & evening except Sat evening, not Christmas or Boxing day): *fresh fish of the day, steak & kidney pie with ale, stag & boar pie, pork casserole with cheese & herb dumplings, sirloin steak. Homemade treacle pudding, rum & raisin pudding. Children's menu.*

Examples from £14 table d'hote (evenings only): *grilled fillet of cod with light curry sauce, roast fillet of lamb carved on ratatouille. Chocolate cherry & cognac roulade.* 'Jewels' menu (lunchtimes also, by request): *breast of Suffolk guinea fowl with mango & stem ginger, beef Wellington, mille feuille of salmon & scallops on lemon cream sauce. Vegetarian menu. Trad. Sun. roasts. Bookings advised.*

Suffolk's 'Best Kept Village' is a title often won by Westleton, with its 14th century thatched church and village green with duck pond. Photographs of bygone years on the walls of the inn show very little has changed, but Rosemary and Richard Price offer 'state of the art' amenities: six Honeymoon rooms, some with four posters or half tester beds, all equipped with superb bathrooms complete with jacuzzi, and over £300,000 was spent recently on the kitchens! Barbecues are held weekend lunchtimes (weather permitting) in the picturesque terraced garden (by Blooms of Bressingham), and a very large conservatory is for the use of non smokers. Inside has an open log fire which spits and crackles on a cold day. Very fresh local fish is the house speciality, skilfully prepared. World famous Minsmere Nature Reserve is just a few minutes walk.

THE WHITE HORSE HOTEL

Station Road, Leiston.

Tel. (0728) 830694
Fax (0728) 833105

Location: On main road into Leiston.
Credit cards: Access, Visa, Diners, Amex.
Accommodation: 4 singles (£33.50), 5 doubles, 4 twins (£52.50), 1 family.
Most en suite, tv's, tea & coffee, phone. 'Let's Go weekend
break £62.50 (dinner, b & b).
Bitters: Greene King, Theakstons Old Peculier, McEwans Export,
Exhibition, Scotch.
Lagers: Becks, Kronenbourg, McEwans, Harp.

Examples of bar meals (lunch & evening, 7 days): *ragout of venison, sweet & sour chicken, steak & kidney pie, seafood pancake, trout, smoked haddock prawns & mushroom tagliatelle, jacket potatoes, salads, ploughman's, daily specials eg steak, cauliflower & brie pie, roast pork. Ipswich almond pudding, real sherry trifle.*
Examples of restaurant meals (as above): *halibut in vermouth sauce, king prawn tails in sweet & sour sauce, steaks & grills, game pie, strips of veal in white wine & cream sauce, chicken breast flamed with Calvados. Trad. Sun. roasts (booking advised).*

Far more attractive inside than out, this 18th-century hostelry is exceptionally well equipped: the astonishing play area in the garden will appease even the most hard-to-please youngster, and parents will appreciate the two bars, restaurant and well appointed bedrooms. Food is of a high order, but special mention must be made of the 100+ illustrated wine list. This wild and beautiful coast is in some ways best seen in winter; John and Jean Doyle offer special Christmas and winter packages, which are very popular. Parking for 16 cars.

THE BELL HOTEL

High Street, Saxmundham.

Tel. (0728) 602331
Fax (0728) 833105

Location: Town centre.
Credit cards: Access, Visa, Diners, Amex.
Accommodation: 3 singles (from £25), 3 doubles, 6 twins (£50), 2 family. Most en suite, tv's, tea & coffee, phone. Weekend breaks £62.50pp (dinner, b & b).
Bitters: Greene Kinng, Rayments, Scotch.
Lagers: Becks, McEwans, Henry Funck.

Examples of bar meals (lunch & evening, 7 days - bar open al day): *homemade steak & kidney pie, pizzas, steaks, curry, gammon, plaice, scampi, salads, omelettes.*
Examples of restaurant meals (as above): *Italian:- fillet steak Napotetana, veal escalopes with marsala, sole fillets in white wine sauce with scampi & tomato sauce, king prawns in garlic butter, pasta dishes, pizzas. Trad. Sun. roasts (booking advised).*

This dignified former coaching inn has been at the centre of Saxmundham life for over 300 years, and since its acquisition by John and Jean Doyle is now sister hotel to the White Horse in nearby Leiston. Those with a taste for the Mediterranean will relish the strong Italian flavour in both menu and wine list, but there are ample alternatives for those who prefer staple English fare. Chef Brian Craven is interested in all types of cuisine, and with wife Sheila he is also the manager. The hotel is well suited to business or pleasure, and facilities are good for both - a baby listening service, for example, and a fully equipped conference room. Weddings are also catered for. Children welcome. Car park.

THE WHITE HART

The Thoroughfare, Halesworth.   Tel. (0986) 873386
    Location: Town centre, at end of main town car park.
Credit cards: Not accepted.
      Bitters: Adnams, Bass, Worthington, Tetley, Stones, guests.
      Lagers: Carling, Tennents, Tennents Extra.

Examples of bar meals (lunch & evening, 7 days except Christmas & Boxing Days):
*homemade pies (steak in ale, gammon & mushroom), casseroles (eg lemon & lime pork,
orange lamb), fresh fish (eg plaice with stilton sauce, cheesy baked cod), lasagne, quiches,
salads, ploughman's, sandwiches. Homemade sponge puddings, apple pies, crumbles. Trad
Sun roasts.*
NB Open: Mon - Sat 11am - 3pm, 6 - 11pm; Sun 12 - 3pm, 7 - 10:30pm.

Barry and Jenny Howes took over this 17th-century town pub in 1990. The
reputation which they have established for traditional home cooking, using all local
fresh produce, is being firmly maintained. They undertook complete refurbishment
in March '91, to make the best of the old beams and inglenooks, and have furnished
beautifully in cottage style. They always extend a warm welcome, children
included, for whom there are smaller portions and a patio to the rear. Before or after
a good meal one could browse through the many quaint and interesting shops in the
pleasant pedestrian thoroughfare. Large pay-and-display car park to rear of pub.
**SPECIAL OFFER: 10% OFF MEALS MON - FRI ON PRESENTATION OF
THIS BOOK.**

THE HUNTSMAN & HOUNDS

Stone Street, Spexhall, nr Halesworth.   Tel. (098 681) 341

Location:	On A144 Halesworth to Bungay Road.
Credit cards:	Mastercard, Visa.
Accommodation:	1 twin, 1 family.
Bitters:	Adnams, guests.
Lagers:	Red Stripe, Carlsberg.

Examples of bar meals (lunch & evening, 7 days): *steak pie, chicken pie, curry, steaks, fillet of cod in savoury sauce, plaice goujons, veg lasagne, ploughman's, sandwiches, at least 5 daily specials.*

Examples of restaurant meals (evenings only, 7 days): *mixed grill, steak Arizona (fillet stuffed with stilton, wrapped in bacon), prawn curry, trout, lemon sole. Trad. Sun. lunch (booking advised).*

Last year (1992) marked the quincentennial of Columbus' rediscovery of America - a turning point in history. Whilst he was so engaged the roof was being put on The Huntsman & Hounds. The sheer size of the oak beams used suggests that the builders fully intended the building to last for at least 500 years, but it is less clear why the ceilings slope so steeply out from the centre. Two inglenooks, back-to-back but no longer sharing the same fire, shed their warmth and light over the bars, reflected in the handsome terra cotta flooring in the Public. Furniture is solid wood and comfortable, and the dining room is compartmented for greater privacy. David and Janet have, over 10 years, acquired a reputation for good food in very generous portions. They welcome children and have a garden with duck pond (and new patio). Private dining room for up to eight people.

THE DUKE WILLIAM

The Street, Metfield, nr Harleston.　　　　　　　　Tel. (0379) 86371
　　Location:　Between Halesworth and Harleston.
Credit cards:　Not accepted.
　　Bitters:　Adnams, guests.
　　Lagers:　Tennents Extra, Carling.

Examples of bar meals (lunch & evening, 7 days): *steaks, sesame chicken goujons, Norfolk jumbo sausages, cod, seafood platter, vegetable grills, salads, ploughman's, sandwiches. Apple pie, gateau.*
Examples of restaurant meals (as above): *steaks, mixed grill, pork chop with apple sauce, honey roast duckling with apple sauce, scampi, plaice, salads. Trad. Sun. roast £6.95 (3 courses + coffee) - booking advised.*

The original Duke William is now a private cottage, just a little distance away. Its successor was built in the 1940's - yesterday in terms of pub antiquity. Yet it achieves a cosy intimacy by a happy combination of beamed ceilings, brick fireplace and bar, lots of brass, cottagey furniture and a green abundance of lovely indoor plants. Landlord Alan Brown has been pulling pints here for three years or so - Adnams (based in nearby Southwold) plus a selection of ever changing guests - and has secured a place in the CAMRA guide. Straightforward food is served in generous portions at modest prices; sandwiches from one pound, two plaice fillets at £4.95 (with all the trimmings), for example. Children are welcome if dining, and the garden has play area and occasional barbecues. Otter Trust at Earsham and falconry at Laxfield within easy reach. Accommodation and caravan site in village.

THE BLACK SWAN

Homersfield, nr Harleston.   Tel. (098 686) 204
Location: Past village green, by River Waveney.
Credit cards: Access, Visa.
Accommodation: 1 family, 1 twin, 1 single.
Bitters: Adnams, Websters, guests. Plus Guinness.
Lagers: Carlsberg, Kronenbourg 1664, Fosters.

Examples of bar/restaurant meals (lunch & evening, 7 days): *full range from simple bar snacks to 3-course dinner eg beefsteak & kidney pie with suet pastry, range of farmhouse casseroles, chicken & broccoli cream bake, mushroom & almond garlic crust pie, fresh fish of the day. Trad. Sun. roast.*

Standing on the Suffolk banks of the River Waveney, The Black Swan is part of a 1,000 year tradition of inn-keeping on this spot. Now by-passed, Homersfield is a quiet, pretty village, well suited to a long weekend away, or as a base from which to explore the rest of the Waveney Valley. Period photographs on the oak-panelled bar record local history, including Flixton Hall, seat of the Adair family estate. All visitors are invited to enjoy the informal hospitality of Bill, Jane, Leighten, Alison and Louise, who continue the famly tradition of fine ale and wholesome farmhouse cooking. The policy of "freshly caught, locally bought and homemade" makes for an abundant choice, from fresh fish to tasty vegetarian dishes. Diversity is also the watchword of the new Band Nights and dinner dances, from jazz to Jagger! In addition to four bars and elegant dining room, there is a games room with pool and darts. The large garden (with barbecue) extends to riverside walks through meadows. Children welcome.

THE CHEQUERS INN

23 Bridge Street, Bungay.   Tel. (0986) 893579
 - Location: On Ditchingham road, near town centre.
 - Credit cards: Not accepted.
 - Bitters: Adnams, Bass, Greene King IPA, Fullers, 4 guests.
 - Lagers: Tennents, Carlsberg Export, Miller Lite. Plus traditional English country wines.

Examples of bar meals (lunchtimes Mon - Fri): *homemade curries, steak & kidney pie, chicken pie, steak & onion in ale, lasagne, fresh fish (Weds), jacket potatoes, doorstep sandwiches (noted), salads, ploughman's, vegetarian.*

Recommended by good beer guides, with dozens of old beer jugs hanging from the beams, Vicky and Dave Godbold's cottagey 16th-century town pub is much more than a mere drinkers' den. Food is all homecooked and hearty, the welcome warm (extended to well-behaved children). There's no food served in the evenings, so this is a time to sample some of the rare and excellent ales (eg Hook Norton, Mitchells of Lancaster), brought here from all over the country, in a conversational atmosphere further enlivened by entertainment laid on occasionally. All are welcome to the regulars' quiz night every Sunday. A covered patio has a barbecue which can also be used for private functions. Bungay Castle and the famous Earsham Otter Trust are nearby attractions. Car park.

THE TALLY HO

Mettingham, nr Bungay.　　　　　　　　　　　　　　Tel. (0986) 892570
  Location: On B1062 between Beccles and Bungay.
 Credit cards: Not accepted.
   Bitters: Courage Directors & Best, John Smiths,
   Lagers: Kronenbourg, Fosters, Miller Lite.

Examples of bar/restaurant meals (lunch & evening, 7 days): *wings of fire, battered calamari, lemon sole, prawns in batter, chicken Kiev, steaks & grills, salads, jacket potatoes, ploughman's, sandwiches, daily lunch specials eg homemade steak pie, lamb & mushroom pie, rustler pie, cottage pie, lasagne; curry, chilli. Homemade fruit pie, Dutch apricot crumble flan, spotted dick, chocolate fudge cake. Children's menu. Trad. Sun. roasts (booking advised).*

A pub that serves food - not a restaurant; that's how licensees Brian and Sylvia Price aim to keep things. There's no waitress service - food is ordered at the bar and brought to your table - and emphasis is on value for money. Customers seem to like it and the EDP gave a very favourable review recently in the Foodfile feature. Built in 1845, the pub was known as The Fox & Hounds until 1885 and has been a shop and wheelwrights (though apparently never having had a connection wih hunting). In a very attractive interior the most notable artefacts are a collection of china - jugs, teapots, plates. These rattle a little every Thursday evening to the lively refrains of the Sole Bay Jazz Band. Well-behaved children are welcome and the garden has swings and climbing frames. Wheelchair access.

THE SWAN INN

Swan Lane, Barnby, nr Beccles.   Tel. (0502) 76646
    Location: On A146 between Beccles and Oulton Broad.
    Credit cards: Access, Visa.
        Bitters: Adnams, Greene King Abbott, Bodingtons, Whitbread Best.
        Lagers: Stella Artois, Heineken.

Examples of bar meals (lunch & evening, 7 days): *skate goujons, smoked salmon steaks, grilled fresh sardines, cod or plaice mornay, crab gratin with prawns, specials.*
Examples of restaurant meals (as above): *smoked sprats, Italian seafood salad, avocado Monte Carlo; prawn & lobster thermidor, crab claws in garlic butter, whole grilled North Sea turbot, wing of skate in black butter, fish of the day, steaks. Trad. Sun. roast £4.95 (1-course). Booking advised.*

Anyone with a penchant for fresh fish should make a bee line for this uncommon country inn; owned by the Cole family, well known Lowestoft fish merchants, its kitchens can call upon the very best of the daily catch. Naturally, the menus are dominated by seafood, but there are always alternatives, plus theme nights such as Caribbean, French or 'Mafia', for example. Live music is sometimes heard on Thursday evenings. The nautical flavour extends to the decor: a boat is suspended from the beamed restaurant ceiling, and fishing nets and the like are used to good effect. The inn dates from 1690, and is said to be haunted by a young child brought in from a nearby train crash in the 1800's. The Cole family also accept live children (well-behaved!) in the restaurant, and have a garden with patio. Aquatic centre in village.

THE PLOUGH

Market Lane, Blundeston, nr Lowestoft. Tel. (0502) 730261
Location: Just off village centre.
Credit cards: Not accepted.
Bitters: Adnams, Ruddles, Websters, Norwich, Courage Directors.
Lagers: Fosters, Carlsberg, Holsten Export.

Examples of bar meals (lunch & evening, 7 days): *homemade soup, breaded mushrooms & dip, lasagne, chilli, scampi, cod, plaice, homemade steak & kidney pie, steaks, chicken Kiev, burgers, filled jacket potatoes, cheese & leek bake, tuna & broccoli pasta bake, prawns & mushroom pasta in garlic butter, salads, ploughman's, daily specials. Banana cheesecake, chocolate gateau. Children's menu.*

"Barkis is willing" and he set off from here on his coach in 'David Copperfield'. Letters still arrive from distant places addressed to Dickens' eponymous hero. The great author must have supped here; built in 1701 it was quite well established even in his time. He would surely find it still to his liking. Original oak panelling and exposed beams together with high back settles and open fires combine most agreeably in the large lounge bar. The public bar has old-fashioned skittles, and children are permitted in the small dining room (booking advisable at weekends). The large garden is a sheltered spot, and just a step across the large car park will take you to the Plough's own bowling green. Pat and Linda are the amiable couple who over eight years have made this unique pub very well regarded in the area - well worth a visit even if you're not a Dickens fan.

THE FERRY INN

Reedham.   Tel. (0493) 700429
  Location: By River Yare, on B1140.
  Credit cards: Access, Visa.
  Bitters: Woodfordes, Adnams, Youngers.
  Lagers: Holsten, Tuborg Gold, Carlsberg.

Examples of bar meals (lunch & evening 7 days): *changing seasonal menu using only fresh produce, with meats from local butchers & hand picked fish from Lowestoft market. Chef's daily specials, vegetarian dishes, salads, fresh filled rolls & sandwiches. Children's menu. Italian menu eg lamb & tarragon pie, baked cod fillet Italian style, pizzas, fillet steak on creamy green peppercorn sauce.*

Very few private ferries still operate, and here is the only one left in East Anglia. It has been carrying vehicles of all kinds since the 16th century, and remarkably is still the only crossing point between Norwich and Yarmouth. The inn is therefore guaranteed fame of a kind, but the Archers, who run both it and the ferry, make it worth a call on its own merit. Apart from serving good food in clean and pleasant surrounds, they are considerate hosts, offering to make up a bottle for the baby and providing changing facilities in the ladies washroom, for example. Older children are well accommodated in a large sun lounge overlooking the river. On a sunny day the table and chairs on the bank are a glorious place to sit and watch the various craft plough the waters, including the ferry itself, ofcourse. There are moorings and a launch ramp, and next to the inn a four acre caravan and camping site, and an interesting woodcraft shop.

THE FISHERMAN'S RETURN

The Lane, Winterton-on-Sea.   Tel. (0493) 393305/393631

Location:	Near village centre and fine sandy beach.
Credit cards:	Not accepted.
Accommodation:	3 doubles, 1 single, from £20 pp incl. Rooms are quaint with sloping ceilings. Tea & coff. facilities.
Bitters:	Ruddles, Websters, Adnams.
Lagers:	Holsten, Fosters, Carlsberg. Plus James White & Scrumpy Jack cider.

Examples of bar meals (lunch & evening 7 days): *Fish pie, Hungarian goulash, mussel & mushroom lasagne, seafood pasta, grilled Dover sole, burgers and steaks (chargrilled), ratatouille with cheese & garlic bread, salads, omelettes, sandwiches, ploughman's, children's specials. Mississippi mud pie, homemade raspberry tart, blackcurrant crumble.*

Converted from 300-year-old fishermen's cottages, this is an extremely popular and deceptively roomy inn. The maritime theme pervades the bars in the form of old photographs and seascapes. In winter the open fires broadcast their warm welcome - the winds off the sea are bracing at times. To the rear a spacious room for families overlooks a patio and garden with swings. There is also a large room for functions, seating 40 or 60 buffet style. This strange and beautiful coast is a marvellous spot to recharge one's spirits, and for a more prolonged stay there are four charming bedrooms, old fashioned but comfortable. All is homecooked to a standard which routinely earns credit from Egon Ronay and other leading guides. Vegetarian dishes have become a speciality. Good choice of at least 20 malt whiskies, 13 wines and champagne. Dart board.

THE LION

West Somerton, nr Gt Yarmouth.   Tel. (0493) 393289

         Location: B1159 coast road.
   Credit cards: Not accepted.
         Bitters: Greene King, Marstons Pedigree, McEwans Export, Sam
                     Smiths,Whitbread Best, guests.
         Lagers: Heineken, Stella Artois.

Examples of bar meals (lunch & evening, 7 days): *half roast duckling in orange sauce, steaks, lasagne, chilli, burgers, pizza, king prawns in garlic butter, plaice, scampi, ploughman's. Cherry/apple tart, chocolate fudge cake, icecreams.*

An underground tunnel leads from the cellars of this 18th century freehouse to the 13th century church just opposite. This would seem to confirm local legends that The Lion was once a smugglers' haunt, as in those days men of the cloth were often 'sympathetic' to the pursuit of contraband. They had some fine beaches on which to land it, still eerily quiet, even in high summer. These days a quite different clientele finds refuge here: anglers rub shoulders with birdwatchers, yachtsmen from nearby Martham Broad and visitors to Horsey Mere with its famous windmill, a mile or so down the road. It's very much a homely, family pub, having a children's room and family dining room. In summer enjoy a relaxed lunch at a picnic table and watch the odd spectacle of yacht sails apparently gliding leisurely through the fields. Sue and Ian Milroy have warmly welcomed many thousands in their seven years here, and have maintained a place in leading good pub and beer guides.

THE HORSE & DRAY

137 Ber Street, Norwich.   Tel. (0603) 624741
    Location: Short walk up from Bonds dept. store, near Ber Gate.
Credit cards: Access, Visa, Diners, Delta.
     Bitters: Adnams (full range), many guests.
     Lagers: Red Stripe, Kronenbourg, Carling.

Examples of bar meals (every lunchtime): *a full menu is available every lunchtime, including freshly prepared homemade soups, curries, lasagne, fresh Lowestoft plaice.*

Winner of Adnams' "Best Kept Bar Award" and "Best Kept Cellar Award" in 1992, The Horse & Dray is a rarity in that customers journey here for beer and conversation, without the intrusion of jukebox or pool table. Licensee Sandy Thompson is a firm believer in the old-fashioned interpretation of the word 'hostelry'; she and her staff greet everyone entering the front door with a kind word and a smile. They offer a wide selection of ales and over 70 malt whiskies, and the warm and friendly atmosphere of this comfortable house. In addition to the sensibly-priced menu, Sandy keeps a good selection of wines, also realistically priced, chosen from the Adnams' range, winners of the 1992 "Wine Merchants of the Year."

NB SPECIAL OFFER: *10% off any bottle of wine to customers presenting this guide.*

THE COACH AND HORSES

57 Bethel Street, Norwich.   Tel. (0603) 631337

      Location: 300 yards from market, towards R.C. cathedral (2 mins walk from Theatre Royal).

Credit cards: Access, Visa, Diners, Amex.

       Bitters: Rayments, Greene King, I.P.A. and Abbot.

       Lagers: Stella Artois, Kronenbourg, Harp.

Examples of bar meals (lunch & evening every day except Sun.): *daily specials, filled jacket potatoes, torpedoes (large rolls with various fillings).*

Examples of restaurant meals (as above): *vegetarian specials, hot tiger prawn tails in garlic butter, barbecued rack of ribs, steaks, steak & mushroom pie, liver & bacon casserole, fisherman's pie, plaice Dieppe, vegetable stroganoff, salads. Raspberry tropicana, combination sorbet.*

This is one of the very few pubs in the region to remain open all day - a welcome refuge from the bustle of the city. But it's not at all a typical city centre pub, rather a traditional country inn - no juke boxes etc., but a relaxed, informal atmosphere and good wholesome food - proprietors Geoff and Mary Slater take care that only the freshest produce is used. One end of the L-shaped bar could be described as a small museum: fascinating old photographs and paintings adorn the walls, and in a glass case is displayed a child's slipper found in the foundations, a 16th century custom meant to bring luck. The Victorian end, as it is called, comprises U-shaped leather conversation seats and appropriate gaslights. This popular hostelry is just a short walk from the market place, behind and to the left of City Hall, and is oft frequented by theatre-goers, stage hands and well-known actors.

THE PARSON WOODFORDE

Weston Longville, nr Norwich. Tel. (0603) 880106
- Location: Just off A1067, opposite church.
- Credit cards: Not accepted.
- Bitters: Woodfordes Wherry, Marstons Pedigree, Bass, Adnams, Beamish stout, guests.
- Lagers: Tennents Pilsner, Tennents Extra.

Examples of bar meals (lunch & evening 7 days): *Traditional homemade dishes, vegetarian, daily specials, ploughman's, salads, Children's menu. Trad. Sun. roasts. (Winter only)*

Many readers will know of the Parson as the celebrated 18th-century diarist, famed for his prodigious feasting and quaffing. For a man of the cloth he had remarkably relaxed views on contraband, even to the extent of burying rum in the garden to foil Customs & Excise. He would be well pleased to have the honour of such a notable establishment, just across the road from his parish church, named after him, and would appreciate even more the victuals served there. The L-shaped bar is constructed, in the style of the 16th century, with exposed timbers and open fires. To the rear a well equipped function room for up to 50 seated - small weddings catered for. Landlady Denise Benton, manageress Christine Lilwall and staff welcome children - the pub is very suitable for families - and have swings in the garden. Large car park. Rated in national guides.

THE MERMAID INN

Church Street, Elsing, nr E. Dereham.   Tel. (0362) 637640
     Location: Village centre, opposite church.
Credit cards: Not accepted.
      Bitters: Adnams, Woodfordes, Bass, weekly guest.
      Lagers: Red Stripe, Carlsberg.

Examples of bar/restaurant meals (lunch & evening, 7 days): *chilli, chicken breast stuffed with prawns & lobster or mushrooms & cream cheese, duck in orange sauce, various steaks, lasagne, trout, cod, plaice stuffed with crabmeat, various vegetarian dishes. Homemade trifle, profiteroles, cheesecake, apple pie. Trad. Sun. roast (booking advised).*

Elsing is in many ways a typical Norfolk village: well spread-out and wonderfully tranquil, lost in the heart of the rolling countryside. No such village is quite complete without its church and pub; conveniently opposite the famous 13th-century church stands an exceptional village inn, very much the junior partner, being 'only' 17th-century. Since December 1992 it has been in the hands of John and Sylvia Smither, who extend a warm greeting to all, although Sylvia spends much of her time cooking in the kitchen. This is no small task, as the menu is sizeable and diverse, yet prices remain most reasonable. The bright, spacious bar is timbered and furnished cottage-style, with inumerable items of brass and copperware and a large open fire. Meals may be eaten in the bar or cosy restaurant. Well-behaved children are welcome and there is a garden. Large car park.

THE KING'S HEAD

Bawburgh, nr Norwich.   Tel. (0603) 744977
       Location: Village centre.
  Credit cards: Mastercard.
        Bitters: Marstons, Adnams, Wethereds, Flowers, plus two guests.
        Lagers: Heineken Export, Stella Artois, Heineken.

Examples of bar/restaurant meals (lunch & evening, 7 days): *homemade pies (speciality), chilli, lasagne, quality fresh & breaded fish, sandwiches, salads, filled French sticks, chef's blackboard specials eg venison, pigeon, pheasant, pike, lemon sole, smoked trout, seasonal shellfish, plus array of Mediterranean squid, sardines, goat's cheese, chicken livers*

How many other pubs do you know of that have four squash courts and a bowling green? However, you don't have to be sports minded to appreciate The King's Head. It's a fine old country pub in its own right, and has graced this delightful little village, just a few minutes drive from Norwich, since 1602 (licensed in 1800). The bar is divided in two by a fireplace open on both sides, and on the walls are mounted old firearms and gin traps. But it is for good food and excellent value that most come here, and which has drawn the attention of national guides. The new chef prepares only fresh produce, cooked to order and served with care. Success has resulted in landlady Pamela Wimmer adding a 40-seater restaurant extension. She welcomes children, and maintains a nice little sheltered garden which is a real sun trap. The large car park is a necessity, as this is such a popular venue for Norwich people seeking recreation.

THE BIRD IN HAND

Church Road, Wreningham.   Tel. (0508) 41438
  Location: Village centre.
  Credit cards: Visa, Amex.
  Bitters: Adnams, Woodfordes, Flowers, Marston's Pedigree,
            Castle Eden, two guests.
  Lagers: Stella Artois, Heineken.

Examples of bar meals (lunch & evening, 7 days): *homemade steak & kidney pie, chicken & mushroom pie, lasagne, curry, scampi, burgers, ratatouille, salads, jacket potatoes, ploughman's.*
Examples of restaurant meals (as above): *steaks & grills, trout with cashew nuts, chicken supreme in port & stilton sauce, surf & turf, salmon steaks, homemade pies, nut roast, cottage cheese & spinach pancakes, salads. Trad. Sun. roasts (booking advised).*

John and Carol Turner arrived here three years ago armed with a training from the British Institute of Innkeeping and high hopes. All expectations have been exceeded, necessitating a staff of 35, including three chefs. To have achieved this in such impecunious times clearly indicates they are doing something right! The large, appetising menus are part of the answer, but the beautiful interior, far surpassing the promise of the exterior, is also quite exceptional. The bar was once a stable, and that special farmhouse ambience is unmistakable; the restaurant is even called The Farmhouse, and is furnished most handsomely. There are occasional jazz nights but always a pianist on Wednesday evenings. Well behaved children welcome, and there's a large garden. Weddings and private parties a speciality. Plans for a large function room and accommodation in 1993. Superb washrooms!

THE COUNTRYMAN INN

Ipswich Road, Tasburgh.   Tel. (0508) 470946

Location:	On A140.
Credit cards:	Mastercard, Visa.
Bitters:	Adnams, Bass, Greene King, Fullers, Whitbread, guests.
Lagers:	Carling, Tennents, Tennents Extra, Tennents LA.

Examples of bar meals (lunch & evening, 7 days): *steak & kidney pie, breast of chicken with ham & cheese filling, steak & onion pie, moussaka, omelettes, burgers, ploughman's, daily specials eg curry, lasagne.*
Examples of restaurant meals (evenings only, 7 days - may also be taken in bar): *avocado with prawns, whitebait, veal escalope, char-grilled steak, scampi, plaice. Trad. Sun. lunch.*

The A140 has been the main route between two of the region's principal towns (Norwich and Ipswich) for centuries, and for the last 400 years The Countryman has been a refuge for the weary taveller. But it is also favoured by locals, who come for good, homecooked food, excellent choice of ales and very reasonable prices. The patio and large garden, overlooking rolling fields, provide a sheltered retreat but in unkind weather one will find the two well upholstered bar areas quite amenable. Seating is arranged in semi-circular fashion to aid good conversation, one topic of which might be the unusual collection of stuffed birds. Guests may eat in the bars or small, attractive restaurant. Bill and Sheila Barclay provide the hospitality, and have done so successfully for quite a few years.

YE OLDE KING'S HEAD

The Street, Brockdish, nr Diss.   Tel. (0379) 758125

        Location: On A143.
    Credit cards: Access, Visa, Diners, Amex.
  Accommodation: 2 singles (£20), 3 doubles (£35), 3 twins, 1 family. All en
                       suite, tv's, tea & coff. Discounts for longer stays.
         Bitters: Adnams, John Smith, guests.
         Lagers: Red Stripe, Carlsberg, Fosters.

Examples of bar/dining room meals (lunch & evening, 7 days): *homemade curries, lasagne, spaghetti Bolognese, steaks, scampi, plaice, cod, vegetable lasagne, vegetable curry, ploughman's, sandwiches. Apple pie, hot cherries in brandy sauce with icecream, cheesecake. Trad. Sun. roasts.*

After 500 years there are tales to tell about this characterful inn: two sections of the lounge ceiling can be removed, facilitating the lowering of coffins which could not manage the narrow stairs! Flowers in either bar are likely to be found lying down, perfumed and facing east - allegedly the work of the ghost of a woman killed outside many years ago. If all this sounds a little grisly, be assured that here is a warm, welcoming hostelry, richly timbered and with a fine inglenook to dispel winter chills. Helen and Dave Dedman have hosted for over four years. A member of CAMRA (who recommend the inn), Dave admits he's a real ale fanatic, and shares the cooking with Helen, using homegrown vegetables. Children welcome. Barbecue in garden. Occasional live music at weekends. Shove ha'penny and other indoor games.

THE OLD RAM

Tivetshall St Mary.   Tel. (0379) 676794
       Location: On A140 south of Norwich.
   Credit cards: Access, Visa, Mastercard, Eurocard, Delta, Switch.
  Accommodation: 5 rooms (inc. 2 suites), all en suite. Satellite tv, trouser
                    presses, hair dryers, direct phones, tea & coffee.
        Bitters: Adnams, Greene King Abbott, Ruddles County, Websters.
         Lagers: Carlsberg, Holstein, LA.

Examples of bar meals (7:30am - 10pm every day): *homemade steak & kidney pie, moussaka, lasagne, chilli, curry, fresh fish, fruits de mer, steaks & grills, burgers, aubergine & mushroom bake, veg lasagne, salads, rolls. Pina colada gateau, Alabama soft rock pie, American style cheesecake.*

No matter at what time, the car park of this 17th century coaching inn seems always to be quite full - even at four in the afternoon! It is without doubt one of the most popular hostelries in the entire region, with a name that goes well beyond. The reasons are not hard to discern: as well as being open all day from 7:30am, the menu is enormous, and comprised of good, wholesome favourites, served in belt-loosening portions and in an amiable, lively atmosphere. Not surprisingly, then, it features in just about every major national guide, a credit to John Trafford, who has built this enviable success over the past six years. Special occasions are honoured - roses for ladies on Valentine's Night, Beaujolais, Mothering Sunday, Halloween and others. Children welcome. Large garden. No expense has been spared to make the newly added accommodation quite superb.

GISSING HALL

Gissing, nr Diss.

Tel. (0379) 77291
Fax (0379) 774117

Location: Off B1134, near church.
Accommodation: 4 singles, 7 doubles, 3 twins, 4 suites. All with private facilities (except singles), tv, tea & coff. Trouser press, hair dryer. From £20pp incl.
Bitters: Adnams, guest.
Lagers: Red Stripe, Carlsberg.

Examples of bar meals (lunch & evening except Mon lunch): *smoked chicken tagliatelle, Gissing pie (chunks of prime beef braised with apricots, raisins, coriander & cumin), grilled dabs with mussels & leeks, homemade bacon pudding with tomato & basil sauce, roast vegetable loaf.*
Examples of restaurant meals (evenings Wed - Sat, lunches by arrangement): *puff pastry case of pigeon & roast sweet peppers on tomato coulis, braised Norfolk rabbit in rich spiced sauce, whole roast codling with clams & rich seafood sauce, h/m olive bread (filled with roast peppers, spinach & gruyere). Pear charlotte in dark chocolate sauce, lemon tart.*

Here is a rare opportunity to experience luxury at an everyday price: from £20 per night is astonishingly good value for such rooms in a listed country house, dating from pre-Tudor times. Each is individually styled by co-proprietor (with husband William) Ann Brennan, alias Ann Roy, a professional artist - original paintings adorn the walls. There are also five lovely acres in which to wander, including tennis courts, croquet lawn and a large, well-stocked pond for fishing. Food, too, is exceptional: only the best is used (much of it from the garden), and bread and pastries are homebaked. The public rooms are quite splendid - a marvellous venue for a wedding reception - and facilities are good for conferences etc. Children welcome. Special evenings (eg Halloween, Guy Fawkes) celebrated.

THE BRIDGE

Castle Street, Thetford.   Tel. (0842) 753236
     Location: On river.
     Bitters: Marstons Pedigree, Websters.
     Lagers: Holsten, Carlsberg, Fosters. Plus Scrumpy Jack cider.

Examples of bar meals (lunch & evening, 7 days): *Bridge busters (French bread filled with steak/sausage/bacon & cheese/veg. sausage), salads, ploughman's, sandwiches, daily specials eg wing of skate, stew & dumplings, chicken supreme.*
Examples of restaurant meals (as above): *fresh oysters, beef & onion with ale (topped with puff pastry), chargrilled chicken breast with spicy barbecue sauce, steaks, vegetable curry, daily specials (incl. fresh fish, 16oz T-bone, steak Diane). Children's menu. Trad. Sun. roasts (booking advised).*

Recently acquired by Beryl and Doug King, ably assisted by son Shayne and daughter Michelle (who helps with the cooking), this 19th-century riverside pub has undergone significant changes since it was reported in our fourth edition. Apart from quite new menus, coaches are welcome, barbecues are held by arrangement in summer, and there's a separate bar for functions, meetings and private parties. Whirring ceiling fans help keep the air fresh, and unusual brickwork and cork are also a feature. Families are welcome and the garden has a play area. Centre Parc is very near, and Grimes Graves, Bressingham Gardens and Banham Zoo are all within just a few minutes' drive. Large car park.

THE CROWN HOTEL & RESTAURANT

Crown Road, Mundford.   Tel. (0842) 878233

Location: Village centre, just off A1065.
Credit cards: Access, Visa, Diners, Amex.
Accommodation: 2 singles (£27.50), 5 doubles (£45).
Bitters: Ruddles, Yorkshire, Woodfordes Wherry.
Lagers: Fosters, Carlsberg, Holsten Export.

Examples of bar meals (lunch & evening, 7 days): *salmon & halibut pithivier, cassoulet of duck (speciality), prawn curry, Chinese beef stir fry, tricolour pasta carbonara, vegetarian dishes, daily specials. Treacle & nut tart, apple bakewell, toffee apple tart. Children's menu.*

Examples of restaurant meals (as above): *stuffed mushrooms in Wherry batter, halibut steak topped with creamy clam sauce, honey & mustard chicken, rump steak, pasta & mushroom bake. Trad. Sun. roasts. Booking advised Fri & Sat evenings & Sun lunch.*

"So long as it isn't illegal or immoral, we will do almost anything to make sure you have an enjoyable time with us." These are the words of new landlord (since October 1992) Barry Walker. It was not always thus: a distant predecessor was obliged to diperse assorted riff-raff who were gathered for the magistrates' court, held fortnightly at the inn. In its time (from 1652) The Crown has also been a hunting lodge and doctor's surgery, and, perhaps uniquely in Norfolk, is built on the side of a small hill, so that one may walk in to the ground floor bar and exit from the first floor restaurant. In between, make sure you avail yourself of the excellent home-cooked fare, accompanied by a good selection of French and German wines, which has already won local admiration. An expansion of the garden is planned for summer, 1993.

THE CHEQUERS

Griston Road, Thompson, nr Thetford.   Tel. (095 383) 360

Location: One mile off A1075.
Credit cards: Access, Visa, Mastercard, Eurocard.
Bitters: Adnams, Bass, guest.
Lagers: Carling, Tennents Extra.

Examples of bar meals (lunch & evening, 7 days): *dish of cockles, hot smoked peppered mackerel, steaks, seafood lasagne, smoked ham, homemade steak & kidney pie, mixed grill, steaks, rack of ribs with barbecue sauce, burgers, seafood platter, open sandwiches (speciality), ploughman's, daily special. Chequers special gateau, cheesecake, fruit pie.*

The chocolate box prettiness of this 17th century thatched cottage causes many a foreign tourist to marvel, and it is enhanced by an idyllic setting amongst tall trees. Parts of the inn date from at least the 14th century, and the tiled flooring, exposed brickwork and timber beams are all original and incredibly well preserved - testament to the careful renovation by Bob and Wendy Rourke when they opened here in 1988. The three bars each have their own character, and significantly different ceiling heights - a headache for those who forget! One may eat in any of them, and there's a snug for children. But many choose to enjoy the rural peace in the garden, and the scene when all the hanging baskets are in flower is a joy to behold. On top of all this, The Chequers enjoys a very good reputation for food. Not one to be missed, even though it is a little out of the way.

THE WINDMILL INN

Water End, Gt Cressingham, twixt Swaffham & Watton.   Tel. (076 06) 232

Location:	Village outskirts, just off A1065.
Credit cards:	Not accepted.
Bitters:	Adnams (inc. Broadside), Greene King IPA, Bass, Norwich, Yorkshire, Sam Smiths, weekly guest.
Lagers:	Carling, Carlsberg, Fosters.

Examples of bar meals (lunch & evening, 7 days): *hot potted shrimps, peasant's platter (quiche), chicken continental, shepherds pie, char-grill steak, pancake rolls (inc. vegetarian), Windmill platter (not for the faint-hearted), king sausages, lasagne, fisherman's platter, Atlantic prawns, scampi, cod, burgers, salads (inc. homecooked ham), ploughman's. Black Forest gateau, deep dish apple pie, knickerbocker glory.*

Being in such a rural location, one wonders where all the customers come from, but clearly to do such a good trade one has to be a cut above the norm. A wide choice of food, reasonably priced, is one reason, accompanied by fine ales and the warmth and bonhomie special to country pubs. This one dates from the 14th century, and the oldest part doubles as a party room (not weekends). Rural artefacts, open fires, wooden settles and amusing old prints set the tone, cosy but never twee. A bright garden room (children welcome) with grapevine provides a pleasant alternative. The vocal refrains of Country & Western can be heard on Tuesdays, Folk on the first and third Wednesday of each month. Pool, darts, skittles and shove ha'penny. Large garden with swings etc. A regular in major guides.

THE HARE ARMS

Stow Bardolph, nr Downham Market. Tel. (0366) 382229
Location: Off A10 between King's Lynn (9 miles) and Downham Market (2 miles).
Credit cards: Not accepted.
Bitters: Greene King.
Lagers: Kronenbourg, Harp.

Examples of bar meals (lunch & evening daily): *homemade chilli, curry, lasagne, steaks, creamy vegetable pie, salads, ploughman's, sandwiches, daily specials eg sea bream in prawn & tarragon sauce, chicken breast in sweet & sour sauce.*
Examples of restaurant meals (evenings Mon.- Sat. Booking advised): *spinach crepe (filled with scallops, prawns & mushrooms in creamy sauce), wild boar pate; salmon fillet coated in creamy prawn & lobster sauce, venison country style, Normandy pheasant, 'Hare Arms' tournedos. Trad. Sun. lunch. Table d'hote Mon - Thurs £15.50 (3 courses). Full a la carte Mon - Sat.*

Pleasantly situated in a small village, this popular ivy clad inn has been recommended by Egon Ronay 11 years running for the delicious wholesome fare, achieving the only star rating for food in Norfolk. Fresh local produce is used whenever possible - crab and lobster in summer, pheasant and game in winter. The high standard restaurant, a beautifully proportioned room, offers a menu of traditional and international dishes changed frequently. The 'Old Coach House' is available for a variety of functions, from private dinner or office parties to weddings (and family use on Sundays). Families are also welcome in the sizeable conservatory or attractive garden. Whatever the occasion, rely on good food and service in this exceptional country pub and restaurant.

THE TUDOR ROSE

St Nicholas Street, King's Lynn.   Tel. (0553) 762824
Location:	Town centre, off Tuesday Market Place.
Credit cards:	Access, Visa, Diners, Amex.
Accommodation:	14 rooms, all en suite, with full facilities.
Bitters:	Woodfordes, Adnams, Bass, guest.
Lagers:	Tennents, Tennents Extra, Carling.

Examples of bar meals (lunch & evening, 7 days): *steaks, chicken Kiev, fresh scampi, fisherman's Whitby platter, mushroom cups, vegetable pancake, salads. Trad. Sun. roasts (booking advised).*

Examples of restaurant meals (evenings only): *daily table d'hote menu & full a la carte specialising in steaks & local fish.*

New proprietors Chris and Grace Fiddaman have not been marking time since their arrival in April 1992. Not only have they refurbished the accommodation, they have introduced live traditional jazz every Monday, quiz nights on Tuesdays, theme nights (eg Halloween, Valentine's), plus barbecues (by arrangement) in the beer garden (ideal for children in summer). This 15th-century former merchant's house is one of King's Lynn's finest, oak beamed and full of character. The upstairs 40-cover restaurant is particularly striking. Tuesday Market Place is said to be amongst the most distinguished squares in any English town, and being just yards away The Tudor Rose makes an excellent base from which to explore both the shops and historic quarter. Rated by good beer and other national guides.

THE FARMERS ARMS INN & RESTAURANT AT KNIGHTS HILL HOTEL

Knights Hill Village, South Wootton, Kings Lynn.　　　　Tel. (0553) 675566

Location:　On roundabout at intersection of A149 and A148.
Credit cards:　Access, Visa, Diners, Amex.
Accommodation:　5 singles, 29 doubles, 11 twins, 7 masters, all en suite & with full facilities (some non-smoking). £63-£75 single, £70-£85 double. Weekend breaks £54 pp per night, bed & breakfast & £15.50 meal allowance.
Bitters:　Adnams, Bass, Sam Smiths, Stones, Ruddles, guests.
Lagers:　Carling, Tennents Extra, Tennents LA.

Examples of bar/restaurant meals (all day, every day): *'Farmers Boots' (deep fried potato jackets with delicious filling), 'Green Wellies' (same but vegetarian filling), gamekeepers pie, steak hogie, barbecued ribs, char-grills, Norfolk kebab, whole lemon sole, scampi, swordfish, cod, chilli, veg. lasagne, salads, cobs, blackboard specials. Mississippi mud pie, lemon lush pie, death by chocolate, luxury icecreams. Children's menu. Trad. Sun. lunch & full a la carte in hotel.*

Part of a unique 11-acre complex, The Farmers Arms was converted in 1986 from 17th century working farm buildings, its rustic origins being quite unmistakable: flint walls, cobblestone floors, lots of 'snugs' (ideal for children), and a super function room in the old hayloft. The food is good and wholesome, very fair value, and available all day! Country music lovers should go along Wednesday nights. Petanque is played in the garden, and occasional barbecues held. Children's parties and wedding receptions are a speciality, and with a very smart hotel, health and leisure club and restaurant on the same site, every conceivable requirement is catered for.

ANCIENT MARINER INN AT LE STRANGE ARMS HOTEL

Golf Course Road, Old Hunstanton.   Tel. (0485) 534411
     Location: Off A149, by lifeboat station.
  Credit cards: Access, Visa, Diners, Amex.
Accommodation: At hotel, 3 singles (from £48), 15 doubles (from £65), 15
                   twins, 5 family, all en suite & with full facilities.
                   Special breaks & reduced rates for children.
      Bitters: Adnams, Bass, Charrington, guest.
       Lagers: Carling, Tennants Extra, plus speciality beers from around
                   the world.

Examples of bar/restaurant meals (lunch & evening, 7 days): *steaks, chilli, chicken tikka, special beefsteak & mushroom pie, burgers, cod, salmon & broccoli bake, vegetable pie, cheesy wedges, ploughman's, daily specials (mostly seafood/fish). Death by chocolate, deep dish apple pie, treacle sponge, lemon torte. Children's menu. Trad. Sun. roasts in hotel.*

The only east coast resort to face west, the views from Hunstanton on a clear day, across The Wash to Lincolnshire, are quite spectacular. This gracious 17th-century country house stands in its own grounds, which sweep right down to the sea. To its rear, 'The Ancient Mariner' captures a little flavour of the 'briney', in part by felicitous use of nets and an old rowing boat mounted over the bar. There is a separate restaurant with conservatory extension and an eating area in the bar (divided by a flint wall) which, like the family room, looks out over the garden. Children have swings for recreation, adults tennis courts. Sister pub to The Farmers Arms (South Wootton) and Windmill (Gt Cressingham).

THE GIN TRAP INN

High Street, Ringstead, nr Hunstanton.   Tel. (048 525) 264

Location: Village Centre.
Credit cards: Not accepted.
Bitters: Greene King, Charrington, Worthington, Adnams, Toby
Gin Trap Own, guests.
Lagers: Carling, Tennents, Tennents L.A.

Examples of bar meals (lunch & evening, 7 days): *homemade lasagne, homemade steak & kidney pie, Norfolk pie, Narborough trout, mixed grills, vegetarian dishes, scampi, home cooked ham, steaks, quiches, ploughmans, plus daily specials e.g. chicken & ham pie.*

Margaret and Brian Harmes took over this 17th century coaching inn in 1987, and have improved comfort without 'modernising'. Countless gin traps have been cleverly adapted as light fittings, and rural implements of all kinds cover the ceiling. The portions served are both generous and reasonably priced, a fact which has not escaped the locals' attention! There are two car parks, one of which has stocks where miscreants were once pelted. This lovely corner of England is great walking country, and the Gin Trap is a much favoured watering hole amongst ramblers (who are politely requested not to enter with muddy boots, on account of a very expensive monogrammed carpet!). To round off the trip, why not combine your visit with a look at the adjacent country and sporting art gallery. Children permited in walled beer garden. Occasional visits from Morris dancers.

THE THREE HORSESHOES

Main Road, Titchwell.
Tel. (0485) 210202

Location: On A149 coast road.
Credit cards: Not accepted.
Accommodation: 1 twin, 3 doubles, en suite. From £19.75pp summer, £15pp winter (two people sharing twin or double). £7.50 single supplement.
Bitters: Adnams, Bass, Toby, Stones, Woodfordes, guests.
Lagers: Tennents Extra, Carling.

Examples of bar/dining room meals (lunch & evening, 7 days): all day breakfast, pan fried liver & onion, steak & kidney/mushroom pie, steaks, curries, chilli, lasagne, plaice, cod, "Yorkie" special Yorkshire pudding, potato cheese pie, broccoli & cream cheese bake, salads, sandwiches, ploughman's, daily specials. Weekend carvery (booking advised).

The name of Keith and Teresa Fiddy will be well known to the many followers they acquired in their years at another well-known Norfolk inn, across the county at Ingham, near the Broads. To anyone who appreciates a good country pub it is welcome news that they are repeating their successful formula here on the lovely north Norfolk coast. As they did at Ingham, so they have undertaken a total restoration of this relatively modern building (1923), on the site of a former Three Horseshoes which was one of many secret retreats where Edward VII had those clandestine liaisons with Lilly Langtry (who lived in Norfolk).

They also continue to offer excellent value for money, both for the homecooked meals and the en suite accommodation, the more so when one considers that this is a prime site in outstanding walking country, situated right on the famous Titchwell Bird Reserve, with golf and sailing also close at hand. The weekend carvery is another very popular attraction, and one is well advised to book ahead.

The single large bar is beamed to ceiling and walls, and a separate dining room seats 50. There's a family and games room, with darts, pool, crib and dice, but definitely no jukebox. Private functions up to 120 people can be accommodated by arrangement - coach parties, too. Children are welcome, of course, and the garden with patio has a play area and overlooks the sea. Dogs are permitted in the bedrooms, but not the pub itself.

As always, Keith and Teresa are ebullient hosts, and are fastidious about standards of hygiene.

The Three Horseshoes, Titchwell

THE KING'S HEAD HOTEL

Great Bircham, nr Kings Lynn.   Tel. (048 523) 265

Location:	B1153, village centre.
Credit cards:	Access, Visa.
Accommodation:	2 doubles, 3 twins, all en suite.
Bitters:	Adnams, Bass Charrington.
Lagers:	Carling, Tennents Extra.

Examples of bar meals (lunch & evening, 7 days): *chicken cacciatore, steak & kidney pie, homebaked ham, steaks, curries, crabs, oysters & lobsters in season, salads, sandwiches, specials eg osso bucco, oxtail in red wine.*

Examples of restaurant meals (evenings except Sunday, bookings advised. Lunchtimes by reservation): *halibut Grenobloise, Dover sole meuniere, brodetto (shellfish in garlic butter), steaks, Scottish salmon, scallopine al marsala, pasta specialities. Trad. Sun. lunch.*

The Royal Sandringham Estate, to which the hotel once belonged, draws thousands of visitors to this lovely part of Norfolk. Birdwatchers, yachtsmen and all lovers of gentle, rolling countryside will find spiritual sustenance in unspoilt nature. Sustenance of a more material kind is the speciality of The King's Head, where food is served in all three bars, and in the rather pretty restaurant. The proprietor is Italian, so naturally children are welcome, and have their own room - there's also a large garden (and car park). Historic Kings Lynn and Houghton Hall are very close by, so one is ideally placed for a protracted stay.

THE LORD NELSON

Burnham Market.   Tel. (0328) 738321
  Location: On Fakenham Road, near village centre.
  Credit Cards: Not accepted.
  Accommodation: 1 twin, 1 double, 1 single. S/c cottage in the village.
  Bitters: Ruddles, Websters, Norwich, Woodfordes Nelson's Revenge.
  Lagers: Holsten Export, Carlsberg, Budweiser.

Examples of bar meals (lunch & evening, 7 days): *homemade soups, mushroom Barrington (stuffed with garlic butter & herbs), Nelson prawns (with grapes in light curry mayonnaise), scampi, daily specials eg lobster thermidor pot, sea trout.*
Examples of restaurant meals (lunchtime 7 days, evenings except Sun & Tues): *some dishes as above, crab & samphire soup, marinated fish, local trout with ginger, steaks, fresh fish, oysters, mussels. Homemade cheesecake, ginger meringue. Trad. Sun. lunch (booking advised).*

Fresh, innovative, and with a strong leaning to seafood best describes the food at this very popular inn (far more attractive than first appears from the road), in one of Norfolk's loveliest villages. Quality home cooking has won a place in major guides and a steady succession of awards. Landlord Peter Jordan not only catches his own trout, but is also an expert on wild funghi. The old barn, now a function room, doubles as an art gallery displaying work by, amongst others, landlady Valerie Jordan. Besides a lounge bar (children welcome), there's a public bar with darts and pool, and a charming little restaurant (no smoking) with good, inexpensive wine list. Barbecues are held on the patio in summer. Nelson was born near here, and several hostelries take his name - be sure to get the right one!

THE THREE HORSESHOES

Warham, nr Wells-next-Sea.
Tel. (0328) 710547

Location: Village centre.
Credit cards: Under review.
Accommodation: 2 singles, 1 double, 1 twin & 1 double en suite, + 2 s/c cottages in N. Creake.
Bitters: Woodfordes, Greene King, guests.
Lagers: Carlsberg.

Warham, Norfolk

Examples of bar/dining room meals (lunchtime 7 days, evenings except Thurs): *Brancaster mussels in cider & cream sauce, Warham soused herring, smokie hotpot, Blakeney Point whitebait, local haddock in cheese sauce, toad in the hole, Binham sausages, poacher's game pie, marshman's pie, Norfolk beef pudding, Warham mushroom bake, Norfolk winter vegetable bake, jacket potatoes, ploughman's. Spotted dick, steamed syrup sponge, Nelson cake.*

This anachronistic 18th-century cottage pub will evoke memories of a less frantic age. The two small bars are totally 'un-modern', to the extent of a 1940s fruit machine in one corner. Bare floors, open fires, old furniture and gas lighting complete the agreeable illusion. A separate building houses a children's room with pool and darts, and an attractive garden borders a stream and the village green. A dining room was added in response to growing demand for fresh seafood at reasonable prices, the house speciality, and the menu has also been extended to include more meat and vegetarian alternatives. Also good value is the accommodation, in a picturebook cottage with roses round the door and working water pump in the garden - an idyllic rural retreat in a timeless flint village.

THE SANDPIPER INN

55-57 The Street, Wighton, nr Wells.   Tel. (0328) 820752
        Location: Off B1105.
    Credit cards: Not accepted.
Accommodation: 2 twins, 1 double. Tea & coffee.
        Bitters: Sandpiper, Adnams, guests.
        Lagers: Red Stripe, Tennents.

Examples of bar meals (lunch & evening, 7 days): *steaks, haddock, plaice, scampi, vegetarian burger, ploughman's, daily specials eg chilli, lasagne, spaghetti Bolognese, steak & kidney pie, tandoori chicken, pizzas.*

The glorious Norfolk coastline has long been a Mecca for birdwatchers, but more and more people are discovering its many other charms. This has resulted in a marked improvement in the standard of food and accommodation, previously quite poor, to meet their needs. Originally The Carpenters Arms, The Sandpiper is a good example. Its origins as early 18th century cottages are unmistakable: a double-sided brick fireplace, rough walls, beamed ceilings and cottage-style furniture, with an interesting collection of plates. Pool and old-fashioned pastimes such as darts and shove ha'penny are there, but tradition yields to occasional Italian or Chinese evenings, for example, and barbecues with disco in summer. Barry and Jean are the innovative licensees; they brought long years of experience here with them in 1984, and have secured a place in a major national good pub guide. They welcome well behaved children (and dogs on leads), and have a large garden. Attractive views over Stiffkey valley. Near Wells-Walsingham railway.

THE CHEQUERS INN

Front Street, Binham, nr Fakenham.   Tel. (0328) 830297
        Location: Village centre, on B1388 between Wells and Walsingham.
    Credit cards: Not accepted.
    Accommodation: Double £30, family £36 per room incl. Tv's, tea & coff.
                     Bathroom adjacent. Caravan & camping site with toilets &
                     water supply (booking advised in summer).
        Bitters: Adnams Best, Woodfordes Wherry, Bass, Highgate Mild,
                     Stones, Toby. Mitchell & Butlers Mild.
        Lagers: Carling, Tennents Extra.

Examples of bar meals (lunch & evening, 7 days): *steaks, mixed grill (speciality -
evenings only), all-day breakfast, fresh-grilled salmon, lamb chops, cheese & broccoli
bake, daily specials eg h/m steak & kidney pie, leek & potato pie, halibut in cheese sauce.*
Available 11am-9:30pm (12-3pm, 7-9pm Sundays): *gammon, scampi, cod/plaice,
omelettes, fresh crab, salads, ploughman's, sandwiches. Trad. Sun. roasts £4.95 (1
course).*

One of Norfolk's finest villages, famed for its priory, Binham is also blessed with one
of the county's foremost freehouses, standing in one acre and open all day except
Sundays. Unusual in that the freehold belongs to the village itself, the 17th-century
Chequers has been ably run since January 1991 by Brian Pennington and Barbara
Garratt, both very experienced. They share the cooking, using only the freshest and
best of produce. Prices are exceptional: a huge T-bone with all the trimmings is just
£8.95, for example. Accommodation is also good value. The building itself oozes
character; of special interest is an engraving of the Battle of Portsmouth, during
which the Mary Rose sunk. Well-behaved children welcome. Indoor games. Large
garden. Occasional music nights (especially in winter). Handy for all the attractions
of this lovely area.

THE CROWN

Colkirk, nr Fakenham.   Tel. (0328) 862172
    Location: Village centre.
    Credit cards: Access, Visa, Mastercard.
    Bitters: Greene King, Rayments Special.
    Lagers: Harp, Kronenbourg.

Examples of bar meals (lunch & evening, 7 days): *mushrooms in garlic, homemade soups, steaks, deep fried cod/plaice, fresh fish of the day, gammon, tuna fish salad, sausage hotpot, vegetarian dishes, daily specials eg pork & pineapple curry, steak & kidney pie, fruity lamb curry, liver & bacon casserole, haddock & prawn cheesy bake, vegetable pasta.*

Folk in these parts seem to be unanimous in praise of their local, and it is hard to find fault with such an honest example of the English country pub at its best. The food is fresh and home cooked, the bar and dining room comfortable and pleasant, and the atmosphere congenial. Traditional games like skittles, shove ha'penny, darts and dominoes provide amusement. In winter, warm the extremities with a good hot meal by an open fire, in summer do the same in the sun on the patio or in the beer garden (formerly a bowling green), perhaps with a bottle of wine from an extensive, personally selected list. Pat and Rosemary Whitmore are your amicable hosts, well established here over many years.

119

THE BOAR INN

Gt Ryburgh, nr Fakenham.   Tel. (032 878) 212
           Location: End of village, opp. 13th century church.
       Credit cards: Access, Visa, Connect.
    Accommodation: 1 double, 2 twins.
             Bitters: Wensum (own brand), Adnams, Sam Smiths, Tolly Cobbold.
             Lagers: Stella Artois, Carlsberg.

Examples of bar meals (lunch & evening, 7 days): *mushroom royale (cooked with stilton & garlic), lasagne, steak & kidney pie, Madras beef curry, salads, steaks, chicken Kiev. Meringue glace, fruit crumble, Italian ices.*
Examples of restaurant meals (as above): *chicken tikka, prawn creole, steaks, roast duck in black cherry sauce, rogan josh, rahmschnitzel.*

The Boar is very popular locally, so best to book for the restaurant, and as all is cooked to order, allow a little extra time to be served at peak periods. Take the opportunity to look around this ancient inn; the cosy beamed bar is warmed by an open fire in winter, and the dining room is also very attractive and spacious. Or stroll the few yards to a lovely stretch of the clear River Wensum, which meanders through nearby meadows. The patio by the car park is a sun trap, but the pleasant garden, scented with roses, provides cooler shade. All this plus a comprehensive, international menu has regularly secured an entry in more than one national guide. A good place to stay a while, and perhaps have your hair styled at the salon on the premises!

THE JOHN H. STRACEY

Briston, Melton Constable.
Tel. (0263) 860891
·Location: On B1354 towards Aylsham.
Accommodation: B & B from £15.50 pp. Two-day breaks all year.
Bitters: Sam Smith, Adnams, Burtons, Tetleys, Whitbreads, John Bull, guest.
Lagers: Skol, Carlsberg, Heineken.

Examples of bar meals (lunch & evening, 7 days): *king prawns, homecooked ham, steak & kidney pie (speciality), lasagne, gammon, steaks, scampi, seafood platter, ploughman's, blackboard specials.*
Examples of restaurant meals (as above): *halibut mascotte, salmon a la Stracey, fillet Mexicaine, chicken Espagnol, duck Normandy, steaks. Trad. Sun. lunch £7.25.*

Named after the former world welterweight boxing champion by a previous admiring landlord, this 16th century inn began as a resting and shoeing place for horses - the old stables are now the restaurant. Those indifferent to sport or history will nevertheless appreciate the home cooked food, served in generous portions - the ham is a favourite, tender and melt-in-the-mouth. For several years now Ray and Hilary Fox have retained a loyal local following, for this is one of the better known pubs in the area. Though on a crossroads, it enjoys a fairly peaceful location overlooking fields, with a small garden (and large car park) to the side. The countryside around here is amongst the best in Norfolk; Stody Hall with its magnificent display of rhododendrons, Blickling and Felbrigg Halls are all nearby. Also, the coast is just a few miles away, so an overnight stop may be in order. Children welcome. Les Routiers recommended.

THE RED HART

The Street, Bodham.   Tel. (0263) 70270

Location: Just off (to the south) the A148. Turn at Gresham sign.
Credit cards: Not accepted.
Bitters: Tolly Original, Tetley, Burton.
Lagers: Lowenbrau, Labatts, Heineken.

Examples of bar meals (lunch & evening, 7 days): *homemade cheese & potato pie, steak & kidney pie, cottage pie, spaghetti bolognese, lasagne, pork & pineapple curry, chilli, steaks, scampi, cod, plaice, salads, ploughman's, sandwiches, special rolls, Friday lunch specials (winter) eg liver & sausage casserole, sweet & sour pork, chicken & mushroom pie. Children's meals. Trad. Sun. roasts.*

Here is one of those timeless brick-and-flint village pubs which are so characterisic of North Norfolk. It began around 1650 as a coaching inn, when presumably this quiet country lane was a main thoroughfare. Utterly without pretensions, it is simply furnished cottage-style, with the main feature being a quite splendid inglenook fireplace covered in antiques, some of which have been contributed by locals. Indeed, the public bar, with its pool table and darts, is well frequented by locals, but the principal attraction must be the fresh, homecooked food, served in huge portions at astonishingly fair prices. Cook is Sally Graver, who, with husband Colin, has served here for over five years - only the fourth landlords this century! They welcome children and the garden has a barbecue. Paintings displayed are for sale. Bingo every Thursday in Village Hall.

AYLSHAM MOTEL & RESTAURANT

Norwich Road, Aylsham.   Tel. (0263) 734851

Location: 10 miles from Norwich towards Cromer (near roundabout).
Credit cards: Access, Visa, Switch.
Accommodation: 2 doubles, 11 twins, 1 family, all with full facilities & phones.
Bitters: Adnams, Smith's Sovereign, Worthington Best.
Lagers: Carling Black Label, Tennents.

Examples of bar meals (lunch & evening, 7 days): *homemade steak & kidney pie, lasagne, curry, chilli, wings of fire with garlic dip, pan fried sardines in rosemary, omelettes, salads, ploughman's, many daily specials eg pork chop cordon bleu, cannelloni au gratin, spinach & mushroom bake, fillet of plaice in mushroom & prawn sauce.*
Examples from a la carte (lunch & evening, 7 days): *whole roast pheasant in port gravy, surf & turf (sirloin steak grilled with smoked salmon pate & prawns en croute), beef stroganoff, grilled whole lemon sole.*

This fairly new addition to the Norfolk scene, though not a pub as such, merits inclusion as a small and friendly family-run hotel, offering good, comfortable accommodation and generous portions of fresh, home-prepared food. The Springalls, themselves local people, have in the past year greatly extended the menu, introduced a no-smoking area, and now have a full licence as a freehouse. It's ideally placed, being just 15 minutes from Norwich, the Broads, Felbrigg Hall and the coast. Blickling Hall and the Bure Valley Railway are virtually on the doorstep. Up to 120 can be accommodated for private functions, social or business, and there are exceptionally good facilities for the disabled. Well behaved children welcome. Garden and ample parking.

THE CROWN

Banningham, nr Aylsham.   Tel. (0263) 733534
    Location: Opposite church.
Credit cards: Not accepted.
     Bitters: Greene King, Tolly Original, guest (in summer).
     Lagers: Castlemaine, Stella Artois.

Examples of bar meals (lunch & evening, 7 days): *mushrooms with garlic & stilton, steaks, scampi, plaice, pizza, gammon steak marinated in cider, chicken qtr in wine, jacket potatoes, ploughman's, daily specials eg steak & kidney pie, Devonshire beef casserole, Italian chicken. Meringue special, Norfolk tart, death by chocolate, bread pudding. Trad. Sun roasts.*

New proprietors (since January 1993) Mark and Jeanette Feneron are keen that theirs should be a family-oriented pub. It is one of the most popular in the area, and although a room is set aside for eating there's inevitably 'overspill', so one may eat in any of the four pleasant timbered bar areas, with fresh flowers and warmed by log fires. The building itself is rooted firmly in English traditions, 17th-century and standing right in the shadow of the church. In a display case is an 1851 bible presented by Rev. Bickersmith, composer of the hymn 'Peace, perfect peace' - appropriate enough in this tranquil little village. There's a family room and garden, and ample parking.

THE HILL HOUSE

Happisburgh.   Tel. (0692) 650004
Location: Next to church, off coast road.
Credit cards: Access, Visa, Mastercard, Eurocard.
Accommodation: Self-contained double, en suite. £30 (£20 as single) b & b.
Bitters: Woodfordes, Adnams, Greene King, weekly guest.
Lagers: Hofmeister, Fosters, Kronenbourg.

Examples of bar meals (lunch & evenings 7 days, except Sun & Mon evenings): *daily specials, lasagne, steak & kidney pie, chilli, local crab, char-grill steaks, salads, carvery bar in summer. Children's menu.*
Examples of restaurant meals (evenings only 7 days, except Sun & Mon): *blanchbait, plaice princess (with prawns, peppercorns & cream sauce), giant crevettes in garlic butter, chicken breast in leek & stilton sauce, steaks with speciality sauces (eg ham, asparagus & cheese). Trad. 3-course Sun. lunch £6.25 (children £3.95). Booking advised.*

This was Conan Doyle's favourite retreat - he wrote 'The Dancing Men' at an upper window overlooking Happisburgh's famous golden sands. It's a remarkable Tudor structure with a colourful history and original dry rot in the timbers! Clive and Susan Stockton took over only in May 1992; they extend a warm welcome to all and offer good value. There's a family room, but the very attractive beer garden by the sea is to be preferred if weather permits. Railway buffs might like to know that what is now the letting bedroom was a Victorian signal box, intended for a coastal line which never materialised. The public bar has a pool table, and the garden room seats 30, ideal for functions, business or private. A very well-liked pub locally, and recommended by national guides.

THE SWAN INN

Ingham, nr Stalham.   Tel. (0692) 81099

Location:	Next to church.
Credit cards:	Access, Visa, Amex.
Accommodation:	3 doubles, 1 twin, 1 family, all en suite & with hair dryer, tv & tea & coffee. From £40 double, £30 single. Spring & autumn breaks £28pp half board.
Bitters:	Adnams Best, Woodfordes Wherry, Mitchells ESB, guest.
Lagers:	Carlsberg.

Examples of bar meals (lunch & evening, 7 days): *deep fried brie with tomato & herb sauce, medallions of beef in marsala & orange sauce, loin of pork in port & stilton sauce, butterfly prawns with garlic mayonnaise, 'The Last Great American Dreamburger', chilli tacos, sweet & sour pork, seafood pancake & lobster sauce, wholetail scampi, vegetable tagliatelle, salads, ploughman's, toasted sandwiches.*

Winner of the North Norfolk Tourism Partnership Award for 1991, here is a measure of the way in which Norfolk pubs have improved in recent times. A few years ago it was more-or-less derelict and forgotten. The transformation has been quite remarkable, and the 14th century thatched freehouse is now one of the most popular in the area, with the added benefit of five high quality bedrooms, all with four-posters, in a tastefully converted stable block.

The renovations have not ruined the character of the pub (originally part of a priory), quite the reverse. The old beams, flint walls, brick fireplaces, wooden tables and old photos all combine harmoniously to most pleasing effect. Neither could one be better placed for the famous Norfolk Broads, the deserted sandy beaches of this wild and unspoilt coast, and the fine historic city of Norwich, with some of the best shopping in the country - altogether, a marvellous place to escape for a while.

New owners Iain and Michaela Kemp (since July 1991) are from Suffolk, and have extensive experience in the hotel business. Michaela will be pleased to welcome you front of house, and perhaps tell you stories about the knights which haunt the neighbouring church, and the tragic tale of a young lad who lost his life trying to scale the tower. Meanwhile, Iain prepares fresh food with flair in the kitchen. Meals are wholesome and served in generous helpings, accompanied by a good range of local beers.

The pub has a family room with children's toys, and a small patio to the rear. Dogs are permitted on a lead. Parking is no problem.

The Swan Inn, Ingham

THE WHITE HORSE HOTEL

4 High Street, Blakeney. Tel. (0263) 740574

Location: Village centre.
Credit cards: Access, Visa, Amex.
Accommodation: 2 singles, 4 doubles, 1 twin, 2 family, all with full facilities. From £30 pp incl. Special winter midweek breaks.
Bitters: Adnams, Boddingtons, Flowers.
Lagers: Stella Artois, Heineken.

Examples of bar meals (lunch & evening, 7 days): *deep fried herring roes on toast, fisherman's pie, sirloin steak, ploughman's, sandwiches, daily specials eg potato & parsnip bake, grilled sardines in garlic butter, lasagne. Spotted dick, treacle tart, bread & butter pudding.*

Examples of restaurant meals (every evening plus Sun. lunch. Booking advised weekends): *seafood mornay au gratin, pork in cider & cream sauce, sirloin steak garni, supreme of chicken bonne femme, vegetarian dish. Summer fruit pudding, veiled peasant girl.*

This Tudor coaching inn became a freehouse in June 1992, thereby able to offer increased scope for ever changing beers, to the eminent satisfaction of locals and visitors alike. Blakeney is surely the region's prettiest village, and the views over the quay from some of the very well appointed soundproofed bedrooms are superb. The intimate little restaurant (converted from stables), overlooking the attractive walled courtyard, has already acquired a worthy reputation for good food, accompanied by an excellent wine list. Another worthwhile reason for a visit is the Gallery room, where is displayed an everchanging stock of paintings, prints and sculptures (for sale), and which doubles as a family or function room. Car parking. No dogs.

THE KINGS ARMS

Westgate Street, Blakeney.   Tel. (0263) 740341

Location:	Near quayside, west end of village.
Credit cards:	Access, Visa.
Accommodation:	Self-contained holiday flatlets, £50 in summer, £30 winter, incl. breakfast.
Bitters:	Norwich, Webster, Ruddles, plus locals eg Woodfordes Wherry.
Lagers:	Fosters, Carlsberg.

Examples of bar meals (lunch & evening, 7 days. All day Sundays & holidays): *homemade pies, seafood pasta, local crabs, mussels, prawns, salads, vegetarian dishes, daily specials. Evenings only: steaks, fresh cod, local trout, salmon, gammon steaks, scampi, daily specials.*

Blakeney would be many people's choice for East Anglia's most picturesque village. Its flint cottages, alleys and courtyards are a delight on the eye, and the views from the quayside over the marshes provide a lovely backdrop. Just off the quayside, The King's Arms was once three narrow fishermen's cottages, but is now one of the most popular pubs in the area, recommended by national guides. Howard and Marjorie Davies left the world of the Black and White Minstrels and My Fair Lady 20 years ago and took over from the previous landlord who'd reigned for 45 years! They welcome children (who have their own room, and swings in the large garden) and even dogs if the bar is not full (which in summer it usually is). Smokers themselves may appreciate the facility of a no smoking room to enjoy the good food. See if you can spot the 1953 flood tide mark on an inside wall.

THE CROWN HOTEL

The Buttlands, Wells-next-Sea.   Tel. (0328) 710209

Location: On tree lined green at rear of town centre.
Credit cards: Access, Visa, Amex, Diners.
Accommodation: 1 single, 9 doubles, 4 twins, 1 family (10 en suite). New residents' lounge.
Bitters: Marstons, Adnams, Tetley, John Bull.
Lagers: Castlemaine, Stella Artois.

Examples of bar meals (lunch & evening, 7 days): *goujons of white fish, seafood tagliatelle, steak & kidney pie, prawn & tomato gougere, grills, omelettes, burgers, salads, sandwiches, ploughmans.*

Examples of restaurant meals (as above): *seafood bouche, smoked sea trout, mushrooms stuffed with chicken pate, lambs kidneys sauted with sherry & cream, roast duck with a sauce of fresh pears & brandy, fresh Scottish salmon poached in dry white wine with green grapes, steaks, Crown mixed grill.*

Proprietors Marian and Wilfred Foyers take the prerequisites of fresh quality ingredients and skilful preparation very seriously, and enjoy an enviable reputation well beyond East Anglia. The menu changes daily and is complemented by a tasteful selection of wines from various regions along with an explanatory map. Children are welcome in certain areas, and dogs permitted. Despite the Georgian facade, the hotel is actually Tudor, and the view from the restaurant is of a lovely green with great mature trees attractively dappling the light. Wells town is quaint and relatively unspoilt, and the beach is superb, backed by quite delightful natural pinewoods.

THE ROYAL HOTEL

Paston Road, Mundesley. Tel. (0263) 720096

Location: On coast road.
Credit cards: Access, Visa, Diners, Amex.
Accommodation: 4 singles, 16 doubles, 12 twins, 2 family. All en suite, phone, tv's, tea & coff. Many with bathrooms and 4-posters.
Bitters: Adnams, Greene King, Sam Smiths, Tartan, Stones, Worthington, guest.
Lagers: Becks, Harp, Carling, Tennents, Warsteiner.

Examples of bar meals (lunch & evening, 7 days): *quarter Norfolk duckling/chicken, steak sandwich, scampi, fisherman's/ploughman's lunch, sandwiches.*
Examples of restaurant meals (as above): *lobster Newburg, baked crab thermidor, whole lemon sole meuniere, Bayfield trout almondine, roast Norfolk pheasant, tornedo a la Royal, kleftico, kebab a la Royal, grills. Trad. Sun. roasts.*

Nelson stayed here for two years as a lad; then it was called the New Inn - despite being nearly 200 years old. His bedroom door bears a plaque but he would scarcely credit the modern amenities and comforts within. He would feel at home amongst the many antiquities; the hotel is known far and wide for its period elegance and charm. The present name was acquired on account of the many royal visitors who dropped by during the 19th century. For many years under the personal supervision of the resident Fotis family, it remains much favoured by visitors to this lovely stretch of coast, as well as the locals. Fresh seafood is naturally to the fore in both restaurant and Nelson Lounge, but there is no dearth of alternatives on a very comprehensive menu. Children's lounge. Function room for up to 500.

From the same publisher......

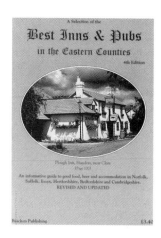

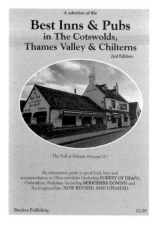

All £2.95
plus 55 pence postage.

Please enclose payment
with order.

Index

BEDS, CAMBS & HERTS

ESSEX

NORFOLK

* accommodation

NORFOLK (Cont)

SUFFOLK

SUFFOLK (Cont)

* accommodation

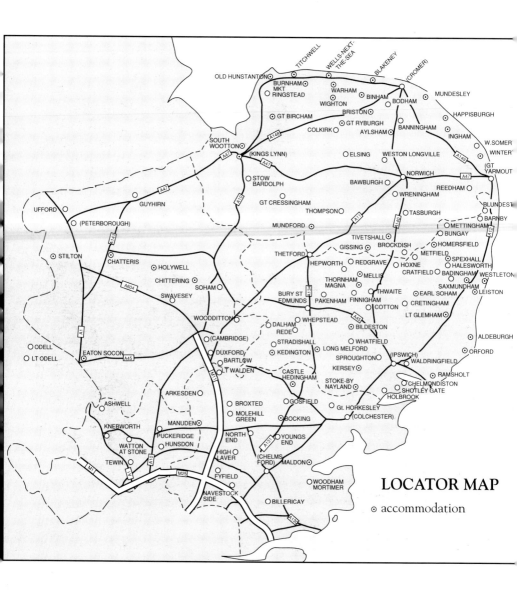

LOCATOR MAP

⊙ accommodation